Two Gentlemen of Verona

William Shakespeare

Akasha Publishing

Akasha Classic Series

Akasha Classics is dedicated to the re-publication of cherished works of World Literature. Many of these writings play a special role in recording the history of human kind, who we are and where we have been.

Akasha Publishing, LLC
877-745-7317
AkashaPublishing.Com

Two Gentlemen of Verona, by William Shakespeare

Library of Congress Control Number: 2009912211

ISBN-13: 978-1-60512-559-6   Hardcover
ISBN-13: 978-1-60512-597-8   Paperback

Shakespeare Titles

Title	Hardcover ISBN	Paperback ISBN
A Midsummer Night's Dream	978-1-60512-544-2	978-1-60512-582-4
All's Well That Ends Well	978-1-60512-545-9	978-1-60512-583-1
Antony and Cleopatra	978-1-60512-572-5	978-1-60512-610-4
As You Like It	978-1-60512-546-6	978-1-60512-584-8
Coriolanus	978-1-60512-573-2	978-1-60512-611-1
Cymbeline	978-1-60512-547-3	978-1-60512-585-5
Hamlet, Prince of Denmark	978-1-60512-574-9	978-1-60512-612-8
Julius Caesar	978-1-60512-575-6	978-1-60512-613-5
King Henry IV, Part 1	978-1-60512-562-6	978-1-60512-600-5
King Henry IV, Part 2	978-1-60512-563-3	978-1-60512-601-2
King Henry V	978-1-60512-564-0	978-1-60512-602-9
King Henry VI, Part 1	978-1-60512-565-7	978-1-60512-603-6
King Henry VI, Part 2	978-1-60512-566-4	978-1-60512-604-3
King Henry VI, Part 3	978-1-60512-567-1	978-1-60512-605-0
King Henry VIII	978-1-60512-568-8	978-1-60512-606-7
King John	978-1-60512-569-5	978-1-60512-607-4
King Lear	978-1-60512-576-3	978-1-60512-614-2
King Richard II	978-1-60512-570-1	978-1-60512-608-1
King Richard III	978-1-60512-571-8	978-1-60512-609-8
Loves Labours Lost	978-1-60512-548-0	978-1-60512-586-2
Macbeth	978-1-60512-577-0	978-1-60512-615-9
Measure for Measure	978-1-60512-549-7	978-1-60512-587-9
Much Ado About Nothing	978-1-60512-550-3	978-1-60512-588-6
Othello, the Moore of Venice	978-1-60512-578-7	978-1-60512-616-6
Pericles, Prince of Tyre	978-1-60512-551-0	978-1-60512-589-3
Romeo and Juliet	978-1-60512-579-4	978-1-60512-617-3
The Comedy of Errors	978-1-60512-552-7	978-1-60512-590-9
The Merchant of Venice	978-1-60512-553-4	978-1-60512-591-6
The Merry Wives of Windsor	978-1-60512-554-1	978-1-60512-592-3
The Sonnets and other Poems	978-1-60512-561-9	978-1-60512-599-2
The Taming of the Shrew	978-1-60512-555-8	978-1-60512-593-0
The Tempest	978-1-60512-556-5	978-1-60512-594-7
Timon of Athens	978-1-60512-580-0	978-1-60512-618-0
Titus Andronicus	978-1-60512-581-7	978-1-60512-619-7
Troilus and Cressida	978-1-60512-557-2	978-1-60512-595-4
Twelfth Night	978-1-60512-558-9	978-1-60512-596-1
Two Gentlemen of Verona	978-1-60512-559-6	978-1-60512-597-8
Winter's Tale	978-1-60512-560-2	978-1-60512-598-5

William Shakespeare
(baptised 26 April 1564 – died 23 April 1616)

William Shakespeare was an English poet and playwright, widely regarded as the greatest writer in the English language and the world's preeminent dramatist. He is often called England's national poet and the "Bard of Avon". His surviving works, including some collaborations, consist of 38 plays, 154 sonnets, two long narrative poems, and several other poems. His plays have been translated into every major living language and are performed more often than those of any other playwright.

Shakespeare was born and raised in Stratford-upon-Avon. At the age of 18, he married Anne Hathaway, who bore him three children: Susanna, and twins Hamnet and Judith. Between 1585 and 1592, he began a successful career in London as an actor, writer, and part owner of a playing company called the Lord Chamberlain's Men, later known as the King's Men. He appears to have retired to Stratford around 1613, where he died three years later. Few records of Shakespeare's private life survive, and there has been considerable speculation about such matters as his physical appearance, sexuality, religious beliefs, and whether the works attributed to him were written by others.

Shakespeare produced most of his known work between 1589 and 1613. His early plays were mainly comedies and histories, genres he raised to the peak of sophistication and artistry by the end of the sixteenth century. He then wrote mainly tragedies until about 1608, including Hamlet, King Lear, and Macbeth, considered some of the finest works in the English language. In his last phase, he wrote tragicomedies, also known as romances, and collaborated with other playwrights.

Two Gentlemen of Verona

by

William Shakespeare

Dramatis Personae

DUKE OF MILAN Father to Silvia.
VALENTINE, PROTEUS } the two Gentlemen.
ANTONIO Father to Proteus.
THURIO a foolish rival to Valentine.
EGLAMOUR Agent for Silvia in her escape.
HOST where Julia lodges. (Host:)
OUTLAWS with Valentine.
SPEED a clownish servant to Valentine.
LAUNCE the like to Proteus.
PANTHINO Servant to Antonio.
JULIA beloved of Proteus.
SILVIA beloved of Valentine.
LUCETTA waiting-woman to Julia.
Servants, Musicians.

[*Scene: Verona; Milan; the frontiers of Mantua.*]

Two Gentlemen of Verona

by

William Shakespeare

ACT I

SCENE I. Verona. An open place.

Enter VALENTINE and PROTEUS

VALENTINE
Cease to persuade, my loving Proteus:
Home-keeping youth have ever homely wits.
Were't not affection chains thy tender days
To the sweet glances of thy honour'd love,
I rather would entreat thy company
To see the wonders of the world abroad,
Than, living dully sluggardized at home,
Wear out thy youth with shapeless idleness.
But since thou lovest, love still and thrive therein,
Even as I would when I to love begin.

PROTEUS
Wilt thou be gone? Sweet Valentine, adieu!
Think on thy Proteus, when thou haply seest
Some rare note-worthy object in thy travel:
Wish me partaker in thy happiness
When thou dost meet good hap; and in thy danger,
If ever danger do environ thee,
Commend thy grievance to my holy prayers,
For I will be thy beadsman, Valentine.

VALENTINE
And on a love-book pray for my success?

PROTEUS
Upon some book I love I'll pray for thee.

VALENTINE
That's on some shallow story of deep love:
How young Leander cross'd the Hellespont.

PROTEUS
That's a deep story of a deeper love:
For he was more than over shoes in love.

VALENTINE
'Tis true; for you are over boots in love,
And yet you never swum the Hellespont.

PROTEUS
Over the boots? nay, give me not the boots.

VALENTINE
No, I will not, for it boots thee not.

PROTEUS
What?

VALENTINE
To be in love, where scorn is bought with groans;
Coy looks with heart-sore sighs; one fading moment's
mirth
With twenty watchful, weary, tedious nights:
If haply won, perhaps a hapless gain;
If lost, why then a grievous labour won;
However, but a folly bought with wit,
Or else a wit by folly vanquished.

PROTEUS
So, by your circumstance, you call me fool.

VALENTINE
So, by your circumstance, I fear you'll prove.

PROTEUS
'Tis love you cavil at: I am not Love.

VALENTINE
Love is your master, for he masters you:
And he that is so yoked by a fool,

Methinks, should not be chronicled for wise.

PROTEUS
Yet writers say, as in the sweetest bud
The eating canker dwells, so eating love
Inhabits in the finest wits of all.

VALENTINE
And writers say, as the most forward bud
Is eaten by the canker ere it blow,
Even so by love the young and tender wit
Is turn'd to folly, blasting in the bud,
Losing his verdure even in the prime
And all the fair effects of future hopes.
But wherefore waste I time to counsel thee,
That art a votary to fond desire?
Once more adieu! my father at the road
Expects my coming, there to see me shipp'd.

PROTEUS
And thither will I bring thee, Valentine.

VALENTINE
Sweet Proteus, no; now let us take our leave.
To Milan let me hear from thee by letters
Of thy success in love, and what news else
Betideth here in absence of thy friend;
And likewise will visit thee with mine.

PROTEUS
All happiness bechance to thee in Milan!

VALENTINE
As much to you at home! and so, farewell.

Exit

PROTEUS
He after honour hunts, I after love:

He leaves his friends to dignify them more,
I leave myself, my friends and all, for love.
Thou, Julia, thou hast metamorphosed me,
Made me neglect my studies, lose my time,
War with good counsel, set the world at nought;
Made wit with musing weak, heart sick with thought.

Enter SPEED

SPEED
Sir Proteus, save you! Saw you my master?

PROTEUS
But now he parted hence, to embark for Milan.

SPEED
Twenty to one then he is shipp'd already,
And I have play'd the sheep in losing him.

PROTEUS
Indeed, a sheep doth very often stray,
An if the shepherd be a while away.

SPEED
You conclude that my master is a shepherd, then,
and I a sheep?

PROTEUS
I do.

SPEED
Why then, my horns are his horns, whether I wake or
sleep.

PROTEUS
A silly answer and fitting well a sheep.

SPEED
This proves me still a sheep.

PROTEUS
True; and thy master a shepherd.

SPEED
Nay, that I can deny by a circumstance.

PROTEUS
It shall go hard but I'll prove it by another.

SPEED
The shepherd seeks the sheep, and not the sheep the
shepherd; but I seek my master, and my master seeks
not me: therefore I am no sheep.

PROTEUS
The sheep for fodder follow the shepherd; the
shepherd for food follows not the sheep: thou for
wages followest thy master; thy master for wages
follows not thee: therefore thou art a sheep.

SPEED
Such another proof will make me cry 'baa.'

PROTEUS
But, dost thou hear? gavest thou my letter to Julia?

SPEED
Ay sir: I, a lost mutton, gave your letter to her,
a laced mutton, and she, a laced mutton, gave me, a
lost mutton, nothing for my labour.

PROTEUS
Here's too small a pasture for such store of muttons.

SPEED
If the ground be overcharged, you were best stick her.

PROTEUS
Nay: in that you are astray, 'twere best pound you.

SPEED
Nay, sir, less than a pound shall serve me for
carrying your letter.

PROTEUS
You mistake; I mean the pound,--a pinfold.

SPEED
From a pound to a pin? fold it over and over,
'Tis threefold too little for carrying a letter to
your lover.

PROTEUS
But what said she?

SPEED
[First nodding] Ay.

PROTEUS
Nod--Ay--why, that's noddy.

SPEED
You mistook, sir; I say, she did nod: and you ask
me if she did nod; and I say, 'Ay.'

PROTEUS
And that set together is noddy.

SPEED
Now you have taken the pains to set it together,
take it for your pains.

PROTEUS
No, no; you shall have it for bearing the letter.

SPEED
Well, I perceive I must be fain to bear with you.

PROTEUS
Why sir, how do you bear with me?

SPEED
Marry, sir, the letter, very orderly; having nothing
but the word 'noddy' for my pains.

PROTEUS
Beshrew me, but you have a quick wit.

SPEED
And yet it cannot overtake your slow purse.

PROTEUS
Come come, open the matter in brief: what said she?

SPEED
Open your purse, that the money and the matter may
be both at once delivered.

PROTEUS
Well, sir, here is for your pains. What said she?

SPEED
Truly, sir, I think you'll hardly win her.

PROTEUS
Why, couldst thou perceive so much from her?

SPEED
Sir, I could perceive nothing at all from her; no,
not so much as a ducat for delivering your letter:
and being so hard to me that brought your mind, I
fear she'll prove as hard to you in telling your
mind. Give her no token but stones; for she's as
hard as steel.

PROTEUS
What said she? nothing?

SPEED
No, not so much as 'Take this for thy pains.' To
testify your bounty, I thank you, you have testerned
me; in requital whereof, henceforth carry your
letters yourself: and so, sir, I'll commend you to my
master.

PROTEUS
Go, go, be gone, to save your ship from wreck,
Which cannot perish having thee aboard,
Being destined to a drier death on shore.

Exit SPEED

I must go send some better messenger:
I fear my Julia would not deign my lines,
Receiving them from such a worthless post.

Exit

SCENE II. The same. Garden of JULIA's house.

Enter JULIA and LUCETTA

JULIA
But say, Lucetta, now we are alone,
Wouldst thou then counsel me to fall in love?

LUCETTA
Ay, madam, so you stumble not unheedfully.

JULIA
Of all the fair resort of gentlemen
That every day with parle encounter me,
In thy opinion which is worthiest love?

LUCETTA
Please you repeat their names, I'll show my mind
According to my shallow simple skill.

JULIA
What think'st thou of the fair Sir Eglamour?

LUCETTA
As of a knight well-spoken, neat and fine;
But, were I you, he never should be mine.

JULIA
What think'st thou of the rich Mercatio?

LUCETTA
Well of his wealth; but of himself, so so.

JULIA
What think'st thou of the gentle Proteus?

LUCETTA
Lord, Lord! to see what folly reigns in us!

JULIA
How now! what means this passion at his name?

LUCETTA
Pardon, dear madam: 'tis a passing shame
That I, unworthy body as I am,
Should censure thus on lovely gentlemen.

JULIA
Why not on Proteus, as of all the rest?

LUCETTA
Then thus: of many good I think him best.

JULIA
Your reason?

LUCETTA
I have no other, but a woman's reason;
I think him so because I think him so.

JULIA
And wouldst thou have me cast my love on him?

LUCETTA
Ay, if you thought your love not cast away.

JULIA
Why he, of all the rest, hath never moved me.

LUCETTA
Yet he, of all the rest, I think, best loves ye.

JULIA
His little speaking shows his love but small.

LUCETTA
Fire that's closest kept burns most of all.

JULIA
They do not love that do not show their love.

LUCETTA
O, they love least that let men know their love.

JULIA
I would I knew his mind.

LUCETTA
Peruse this paper, madam.

JULIA
'To Julia.' Say, from whom?

LUCETTA
That the contents will show.

JULIA
Say, say, who gave it thee?

LUCETTA
Valentine's page; and sent, I think, from Proteus.
He would have given it you; but I, being in the way,
Did in your name receive it: pardon the
fault I pray.

JULIA
Now, by my modesty, a goodly broker!
Dare you presume to harbour wanton lines?
To whisper and conspire against my youth?
Now, trust me, 'tis an office of great worth
And you an officer fit for the place.
Or else return no more into my sight.

LUCETTA
To plead for love deserves more fee than hate.

JULIA
Will ye be gone?

LUCETTA
That you may ruminate.

Exit

JULIA
And yet I would I had o'erlooked the letter:
It were a shame to call her back again
And pray her to a fault for which I chid her.
What a fool is she, that knows I am a maid,
And would not force the letter to my view!
Since maids, in modesty, say 'no' to that
Which they would have the profferer construe 'ay.'
Fie, fie, how wayward is this foolish love
That, like a testy babe, will scratch the nurse
And presently all humbled kiss the rod!
How churlishly I chid Lucetta hence,
When willingly I would have had her here!
How angerly I taught my brow to frown,
When inward joy enforced my heart to smile!
My penance is to call Lucetta back
And ask remission for my folly past.
What ho! Lucetta!

Re-enter LUCETTA

LUCETTA
What would your ladyship?

JULIA
Is't near dinner-time?

LUCETTA
I would it were,
That you might kill your stomach on your meat
And not upon your maid.

JULIA
What is't that you took up so gingerly?

LUCETTA
Nothing.

JULIA
Why didst thou stoop, then?

LUCETTA
To take a paper up that I let fall.

JULIA
And is that paper nothing?

LUCETTA
Nothing concerning me.

JULIA
Then let it lie for those that it concerns.

LUCETTA
Madam, it will not lie where it concerns
Unless it have a false interpeter.

JULIA
Some love of yours hath writ to you in rhyme.

LUCETTA
That I might sing it, madam, to a tune.
Give me a note: your ladyship can set.

JULIA
As little by such toys as may be possible.
Best sing it to the tune of 'Light o' love.'

LUCETTA
It is too heavy for so light a tune.

JULIA
Heavy! belike it hath some burden then?

LUCETTA
Ay, and melodious were it, would you sing it.

JULIA
And why not you?

LUCETTA
I cannot reach so high.

JULIA
Let's see your song. How now, minion!

LUCETTA
Keep tune there still, so you will sing it out:
And yet methinks I do not like this tune.

JULIA
You do not?

LUCETTA
No, madam; it is too sharp.

JULIA
You, minion, are too saucy.

LUCETTA
Nay, now you are too flat
And mar the concord with too harsh a descant:
There wanteth but a mean to fill your song.

JULIA
The mean is drown'd with your unruly bass.

LUCETTA
Indeed, I bid the base for Proteus.

JULIA
This babble shall not henceforth trouble me.
Here is a coil with protestation!

Tears the letter

Go get you gone, and let the papers lie:
You would be fingering them, to anger me.

LUCETTA
She makes it strange; but she would be best pleased
To be so anger'd with another letter.

Exit

JULIA
Nay, would I were so anger'd with the same!
O hateful hands, to tear such loving words!
Injurious wasps, to feed on such sweet honey
And kill the bees that yield it with your stings!
I'll kiss each several paper for amends.
Look, here is writ 'kind Julia.' Unkind Julia!
As in revenge of thy ingratitude,
I throw thy name against the bruising stones,
Trampling contemptuously on thy disdain.
And here is writ 'love-wounded Proteus.'
Poor wounded name! my bosom as a bed
Shall lodge thee till thy wound be thoroughly heal'd;
And thus I search it with a sovereign kiss.
But twice or thrice was 'Proteus' written down.
Be calm, good wind, blow not a word away
Till I have found each letter in the letter,
Except mine own name: that some whirlwind bear
Unto a ragged fearful-hanging rock
And throw it thence into the raging sea!
Lo, here in one line is his name twice writ,
'Poor forlorn Proteus, passionate Proteus,
To the sweet Julia:' that I'll tear away.

And yet I will not, sith so prettily
He couples it to his complaining names.
Thus will I fold them one on another:
Now kiss, embrace, contend, do what you will.

Re-enter LUCETTA

LUCETTA
Madam,
Dinner is ready, and your father stays.

JULIA
Well, let us go.

LUCETTA
What, shall these papers lie like tell-tales here?

JULIA
If you respect them, best to take them up.

LUCETTA
Nay, I was taken up for laying them down:
Yet here they shall not lie, for catching cold.

JULIA
I see you have a month's mind to them.

LUCETTA
Ay, madam, you may say what sights you see;
I see things too, although you judge I wink.

JULIA
Come, come; will't please you go?

Exeunt

SCENE III. The same. ANTONIO's house.

Enter ANTONIO and PANTHINO

ANTONIO
Tell me, Panthino, what sad talk was that
Wherewith my brother held you in the cloister?

PANTHINO
'Twas of his nephew Proteus, your son.

ANTONIO
Why, what of him?

PANTHINO
He wonder'd that your lordship
Would suffer him to spend his youth at home,
While other men, of slender reputation,
Put forth their sons to seek preferment out:
Some to the wars, to try their fortune there;
Some to discover islands far away;
Some to the studious universities.
For any or for all these exercises,
He said that Proteus your son was meet,
And did request me to importune you
To let him spend his time no more at home,
Which would be great impeachment to his age,
In having known no travel in his youth.

ANTONIO
Nor need'st thou much importune me to that
Whereon this month I have been hammering.
I have consider'd well his loss of time
And how he cannot be a perfect man,
Not being tried and tutor'd in the world:
Experience is by industry achieved
And perfected by the swift course of time.
Then tell me, whither were I best to send him?

PANTHINO
I think your lordship is not ignorant
How his companion, youthful Valentine,
Attends the emperor in his royal court.

ANTONIO
I know it well.

PANTHINO
'Twere good, I think, your lordship sent him thither:
There shall he practise tilts and tournaments,
Hear sweet discourse, converse with noblemen.
And be in eye of every exercise
Worthy his youth and nobleness of birth.

ANTONIO
I like thy counsel; well hast thou advised:
And that thou mayst perceive how well I like it,
The execution of it shall make known.
Even with the speediest expedition
I will dispatch him to the emperor's court.

PANTHINO
To-morrow, may it please you, Don Alphonso,
With other gentlemen of good esteem,
Are journeying to salute the emperor
And to commend their service to his will.

ANTONIO
Good company; with them shall Proteus go:
And, in good time! now will we break with him.

Enter PROTEUS

PROTEUS
Sweet love! sweet lines! sweet life!
Here is her hand, the agent of her heart;
Here is her oath for love, her honour's pawn.

O, that our fathers would applaud our loves,
To seal our happiness with their consents!
O heavenly Julia!

ANTONIO
How now! what letter are you reading there?

PROTEUS
May't please your lordship, 'tis a word or two
Of commendations sent from Valentine,
Deliver'd by a friend that came from him.

ANTONIO
Lend me the letter; let me see what news.

PROTEUS
There is no news, my lord, but that he writes
How happily he lives, how well beloved
And daily graced by the emperor;
Wishing me with him, partner of his fortune.

ANTONIO
And how stand you affected to his wish?

PROTEUS
As one relying on your lordship's will
And not depending on his friendly wish.

ANTONIO
My will is something sorted with his wish.
Muse not that I thus suddenly proceed;
For what I will, I will, and there an end.
I am resolved that thou shalt spend some time
With Valentinus in the emperor's court:
What maintenance he from his friends receives,
Like exhibition thou shalt have from me.
To-morrow be in readiness to go:
Excuse it not, for I am peremptory.

PROTEUS
My lord, I cannot be so soon provided:
Please you, deliberate a day or two.

ANTONIO
Look, what thou want'st shall be sent after thee:
No more of stay! to-morrow thou must go.
Come on, Panthino: you shall be employ'd
To hasten on his expedition.

Exeunt ANTONIO and PANTHINO

PROTEUS
Thus have I shunn'd the fire for fear of burning,
And drench'd me in the sea, where I am drown'd.
I fear'd to show my father Julia's letter,
Lest he should take exceptions to my love;
And with the vantage of mine own excuse
Hath he excepted most against my love.
O, how this spring of love resembleth
The uncertain glory of an April day,
Which now shows all the beauty of the sun,
And by and by a cloud takes all away!

Re-enter PANTHINO

PANTHINO
Sir Proteus, your father calls for you:
He is in haste; therefore, I pray you to go.

PROTEUS
Why, this it is: my heart accords thereto,
And yet a thousand times it answers 'no.'

Exeunt

ACT II

SCENE I. Milan. The DUKE's palace.

Enter VALENTINE and SPEED

SPEED
Sir, your glove.

VALENTINE
Not mine; my gloves are on.

SPEED
Why, then, this may be yours, for this is but one.

VALENTINE
Ha! let me see: ay, give it me, it's mine:
Sweet ornament that decks a thing divine!
Ah, Silvia, Silvia!

SPEED
Madam Silvia! Madam Silvia!

VALENTINE
How now, sirrah?

SPEED
She is not within hearing, sir.

VALENTINE
Why, sir, who bade you call her?

SPEED
Your worship, sir; or else I mistook.

VALENTINE
Well, you'll still be too forward.

SPEED
And yet I was last chidden for being too slow.

VALENTINE
Go to, sir: tell me, do you know Madam Silvia?

SPEED
She that your worship loves?

VALENTINE
Why, how know you that I am in love?

SPEED
Marry, by these special marks: first, you have
learned, like Sir Proteus, to wreathe your arms,
like a malecontent; to relish a love-song, like a
robin-redbreast; to walk alone, like one that had
the pestilence; to sigh, like a school-boy that had
lost his A B C; to weep, like a young wench that had
buried her grandam; to fast, like one that takes
diet; to watch like one that fears robbing; to
speak puling, like a beggar at Hallowmas. You were
wont, when you laughed, to crow like a cock; when
you
walked, to walk like one of the lions; when you
fasted, it was presently after dinner; when you
looked sadly, it was for want of money: and now you
are metamorphosed with a mistress, that, when I look
on you, I can hardly think you my master.

VALENTINE
Are all these things perceived in me?

SPEED
They are all perceived without ye.

VALENTINE
Without me? they cannot.

SPEED
Without you? nay, that's certain, for, without you
were so simple, none else would: but you are so
without these follies, that these follies are within
you and shine through you like the water in an
urinal, that not an eye that sees you but is a
physician to comment on your malady.

VALENTINE
But tell me, dost thou know my lady Silvia?

SPEED
She that you gaze on so as she sits at supper?

VALENTINE
Hast thou observed that? even she, I mean.

SPEED
Why, sir, I know her not.

VALENTINE
Dost thou know her by my gazing on her, and yet
knowest her not?

SPEED
Is she not hard-favoured, sir?

VALENTINE
Not so fair, boy, as well-favoured.

SPEED
Sir, I know that well enough.

VALENTINE
What dost thou know?

SPEED
That she is not so fair as, of you, well-favoured.

VALENTINE
I mean that her beauty is exquisite, but her favour infinite.

SPEED
That's because the one is painted and the other out of all count.

VALENTINE
How painted? and how out of count?

SPEED
Marry, sir, so painted, to make her fair, that no man counts of her beauty.

VALENTINE
How esteemest thou me? I account of her beauty.

SPEED
You never saw her since she was deformed.

VALENTINE
How long hath she been deformed?

SPEED
Ever since you loved her.

VALENTINE
I have loved her ever since I saw her; and still I see her beautiful.

SPEED
If you love her, you cannot see her.

VALENTINE
Why?

SPEED
Because Love is blind. O, that you had mine eyes;
or your own eyes had the lights they were wont to
have when you chid at Sir Proteus for going
ungartered!

VALENTINE
What should I see then?

SPEED
Your own present folly and her passing deformity:
for he, being in love, could not see to garter his
hose, and you, being in love, cannot see to put on
your hose.

VALENTINE
Belike, boy, then, you are in love; for last
morning you could not see to wipe my shoes.

SPEED
True, sir; I was in love with my bed: I thank you,
you swinged me for my love, which makes me the
bolder to chide you for yours.

VALENTINE
In conclusion, I stand affected to her.

SPEED
I would you were set, so your affection would cease.

VALENTINE
Last night she enjoined me to write some lines to
one she loves.

SPEED
And have you?

VALENTINE
I have.

SPEED
Are they not lamely writ?

VALENTINE
No, boy, but as well as I can do them. Peace!
here she comes.

SPEED
[Aside] O excellent motion! O exceeding puppet!
Now will he interpret to her.

Enter SILVIA

VALENTINE
Madam and mistress, a thousand good-morrows.

SPEED
[Aside] O, give ye good even! here's a million of
manners.

SILVIA
Sir Valentine and servant, to you two thousand.

SPEED
[Aside] He should give her interest and she gives it
him.

VALENTINE
As you enjoin'd me, I have writ your letter
Unto the secret nameless friend of yours;
Which I was much unwilling to proceed in
But for my duty to your ladyship.

SILVIA
I thank you gentle servant: 'tis very clerkly done.

VALENTINE
Now trust me, madam, it came hardly off;

For being ignorant to whom it goes
I writ at random, very doubtfully.

SILVIA
Perchance you think too much of so much pains?

VALENTINE
No, madam; so it stead you, I will write
Please you command, a thousand times as much; And
yet--

SILVIA
A pretty period! Well, I guess the sequel;
And yet I will not name it; and yet I care not;
And yet take this again; and yet I thank you,
Meaning henceforth to trouble you no more.

SPEED
[Aside] And yet you will; and yet another 'yet.'

VALENTINE
What means your ladyship? do you not like it?

SILVIA
Yes, yes; the lines are very quaintly writ;
But since unwillingly, take them again.
Nay, take them.

VALENTINE
Madam, they are for you.

SILVIA
Ay, ay: you writ them, sir, at my request;
But I will none of them; they are for you;
I would have had them writ more movingly.

VALENTINE
Please you, I'll write your ladyship another.

SILVIA
And when it's writ, for my sake read it over,
And if it please you, so; if not, why, so.

VALENTINE
If it please me, madam, what then?

SILVIA
Why, if it please you, take it for your labour:
And so, good morrow, servant.

Exit

SPEED
O jest unseen, inscrutable, invisible,
As a nose on a man's face, or a weathercock on a
steeple!
My master sues to her, and she hath
taught her suitor,
He being her pupil, to become her tutor.
O excellent device! was there ever heard a better,
That my master, being scribe, to himself should write
the letter?

VALENTINE
How now, sir? what are you reasoning with yourself?

SPEED
Nay, I was rhyming: 'tis you that have the reason.

VALENTINE
To do what?

SPEED
To be a spokesman for Madam Silvia.

VALENTINE
To whom?

SPEED
To yourself: why, she wooes you by a figure.

VALENTINE
What figure?

SPEED
By a letter, I should say.

VALENTINE
Why, she hath not writ to me?

SPEED
What need she, when she hath made you write to
yourself? Why, do you not perceive the jest?

VALENTINE
No, believe me.

SPEED
No believing you, indeed, sir. But did you perceive
her earnest?

VALENTINE
She gave me none, except an angry word.

SPEED
Why, she hath given you a letter.

VALENTINE
That's the letter I writ to her friend.

SPEED
And that letter hath she delivered, and there an end.

VALENTINE
I would it were no worse.

SPEED
I'll warrant you, 'tis as well:
For often have you writ to her, and she, in modesty,
Or else for want of idle time, could not again reply;
Or fearing else some messenger that might her mind
discover,
Herself hath taught her love himself to write unto her
lover.
All this I speak in print, for in print I found it.
Why muse you, sir? 'tis dinner-time.

VALENTINE
I have dined.

SPEED
Ay, but hearken, sir; though the chameleon Love can
feed on the air, I am one that am nourished by my
victuals, and would fain have meat. O, be not like
your mistress; be moved, be moved.

Exeunt

SCENE II. Verona. JULIA'S house.

Enter PROTEUS and JULIA

PROTEUS
Have patience, gentle Julia.

JULIA
I must, where is no remedy.

PROTEUS
When possibly I can, I will return.

JULIA
If you turn not, you will return the sooner.
Keep this remembrance for thy Julia's sake.

Giving a ring

PROTEUS
Why then, we'll make exchange; here, take you this.

JULIA
And seal the bargain with a holy kiss.

PROTEUS
Here is my hand for my true constancy;
And when that hour o'erslips me in the day
Wherein I sigh not, Julia, for thy sake,
The next ensuing hour some foul mischance
Torment me for my love's forgetfulness!
My father stays my coming; answer not;
The tide is now: nay, not thy tide of tears;
That tide will stay me longer than I should.
Julia, farewell!

Exit JULIA

What, gone without a word?
Ay, so true love should do: it cannot speak;
For truth hath better deeds than words to grace it.

Enter PANTHINO

PANTHINO
Sir Proteus, you are stay'd for.

PROTEUS
Go; I come, I come.
Alas! this parting strikes poor lovers dumb.

Exeunt

SCENE III. The same. A street.

Enter LAUNCE, leading a dog

LAUNCE

Nay, 'twill be this hour ere I have done weeping;
all the kind of the Launces have this very fault. I
have received my proportion, like the prodigious
son, and am going with Sir Proteus to the Imperial's
court. I think Crab, my dog, be the sourest-natured
dog that lives: my mother weeping, my father
wailing, my sister crying, our maid howling, our cat
wringing her hands, and all our house in a great
perplexity, yet did not this cruel-hearted cur shed
one tear: he is a stone, a very pebble stone, and
has no more pity in him than a dog: a Jew would have
wept to have seen our parting; why, my grandam,
having no eyes, look you, wept herself blind at my
parting. Nay, I'll show you the manner of it. This
shoe is my father: no, this left shoe is my father:
no, no, this left shoe is my mother: nay, that
cannot be so neither: yes, it is so, it is so, it
hath the worser sole. This shoe, with the hole in
it, is my mother, and this my father; a vengeance
on't! there 'tis: now, sit, this staff is my
sister, for, look you, she is as white as a lily and
as small as a wand: this hat is Nan, our maid: I
am the dog: no, the dog is himself, and I am the
dog--Oh! the dog is me, and I am myself; ay, so,
so. Now come I to my father; Father, your blessing:
now should not the shoe speak a word for weeping:
now should I kiss my father; well, he weeps on. Now
come I to my mother: O, that she could speak now
like a wood woman! Well, I kiss her; why, there
'tis; here's my mother's breath up and down. Now
come I to my sister; mark the moan she makes. Now
the dog all this while sheds not a tear nor speaks a
word; but see how I lay the dust with my tears.

Enter PANTHINO

PANTHINO
Launce, away, away, aboard! thy master is shipped
and thou art to post after with oars. What's the
matter? why weepest thou, man? Away, ass! You'll
lose the tide, if you tarry any longer.

LAUNCE
It is no matter if the tied were lost; for it is the
unkindest tied that ever any man tied.

PANTHINO
What's the unkindest tide?

LAUNCE
Why, he that's tied here, Crab, my dog.

PANTHINO
Tut, man, I mean thou'lt lose the flood, and, in
losing the flood, lose thy voyage, and, in losing
thy voyage, lose thy master, and, in losing thy
master, lose thy service, and, in losing thy
service,--Why dost thou stop my mouth?

LAUNCE
For fear thou shouldst lose thy tongue.

PANTHINO
Where should I lose my tongue?

LAUNCE
In thy tale.

PANTHINO
In thy tail!

LAUNCE
Lose the tide, and the voyage, and the master, and
the service, and the tied! Why, man, if the river
were dry, I am able to fill it with my tears; if the
wind were down, I could drive the boat with my sighs.

PANTHINO
Come, come away, man; I was sent to call thee.

LAUNCE
Sir, call me what thou darest.

PANTHINO
Wilt thou go?

LAUNCE
Well, I will go.

Exeunt

SCENE IV. Milan. The DUKE's palace.

Enter SILVIA, VALENTINE, THURIO, and SPEED

SILVIA
Servant!

VALENTINE
Mistress?

SPEED
Master, Sir Thurio frowns on you.

VALENTINE
Ay, boy, it's for love.

SPEED
Not of you.

VALENTINE
Of my mistress, then.

SPEED
'Twere good you knocked him.

Exit

SILVIA
Servant, you are sad.

VALENTINE
Indeed, madam, I seem so.

THURIO
Seem you that you are not?

VALENTINE
Haply I do.

THURIO
So do counterfeits.

VALENTINE
So do you.

THURIO
What seem I that I am not?

VALENTINE
Wise.

THURIO
What instance of the contrary?

VALENTINE
Your folly.

THURIO
And how quote you my folly?

VALENTINE
I quote it in your jerkin.

THURIO
My jerkin is a doublet.

VALENTINE
Well, then, I'll double your folly.

THURIO
How?

SILVIA
What, angry, Sir Thurio! do you change colour?

VALENTINE
Give him leave, madam; he is a kind of chameleon.

THURIO
That hath more mind to feed on your blood than live
in your air.

VALENTINE
You have said, sir.

THURIO
Ay, sir, and done too, for this time.

VALENTINE
I know it well, sir; you always end ere you begin.

SILVIA
A fine volley of words, gentlemen, and quickly shot off.

VALENTINE
'Tis indeed, madam; we thank the giver.

SILVIA
Who is that, servant?

VALENTINE
Yourself, sweet lady; for you gave the fire. Sir
Thurio borrows his wit from your ladyship's looks,
and spends what he borrows kindly in your company.

THURIO
Sir, if you spend word for word with me, I shall
make your wit bankrupt.

VALENTINE
I know it well, sir; you have an exchequer of words,
and, I think, no other treasure to give your
followers, for it appears by their bare liveries,
that they live by your bare words.

SILVIA
No more, gentlemen, no more:--here comes my father.

Enter DUKE

DUKE
Now, daughter Silvia, you are hard beset.
Sir Valentine, your father's in good health:
What say you to a letter from your friends
Of much good news?

VALENTINE
My lord, I will be thankful.
To any happy messenger from thence.

DUKE
Know ye Don Antonio, your countryman?

VALENTINE
Ay, my good lord, I know the gentleman
To be of worth and worthy estimation
And not without desert so well reputed.

DUKE
Hath he not a son?

VALENTINE
Ay, my good lord; a son that well deserves
The honour and regard of such a father.

DUKE
You know him well?

VALENTINE
I know him as myself; for from our infancy
We have conversed and spent our hours together:
And though myself have been an idle truant,
Omitting the sweet benefit of time
To clothe mine age with angel-like perfection,

Yet hath Sir Proteus, for that's his name,
Made use and fair advantage of his days;
His years but young, but his experience old;
His head unmellow'd, but his judgment ripe;
And, in a word, for far behind his worth
Comes all the praises that I now bestow,
He is complete in feature and in mind
With all good grace to grace a gentleman.

DUKE
Beshrew me, sir, but if he make this good,
He is as worthy for an empress' love
As meet to be an emperor's counsellor.
Well, sir, this gentleman is come to me,
With commendation from great potentates;
And here he means to spend his time awhile:
I think 'tis no unwelcome news to you.

VALENTINE
Should I have wish'd a thing, it had been he.

DUKE
Welcome him then according to his worth.
Silvia, I speak to you, and you, Sir Thurio;
For Valentine, I need not cite him to it:
I will send him hither to you presently.

Exit

VALENTINE
This is the gentleman I told your ladyship
Had come along with me, but that his mistress
Did hold his eyes lock'd in her crystal looks.

SILVIA
Belike that now she hath enfranchised them
Upon some other pawn for fealty.

VALENTINE
Nay, sure, I think she holds them prisoners still.

SILVIA
Nay, then he should be blind; and, being blind
How could he see his way to seek out you?

VALENTINE
Why, lady, Love hath twenty pair of eyes.

THURIO
They say that Love hath not an eye at all.

VALENTINE
To see such lovers, Thurio, as yourself:
Upon a homely object Love can wink.

SILVIA
Have done, have done; here comes the gentleman.

Exit THURIO

Enter PROTEUS

VALENTINE
Welcome, dear Proteus! Mistress, I beseech you,
Confirm his welcome with some special favour.

SILVIA
His worth is warrant for his welcome hither,
If this be he you oft have wish'd to hear from.

VALENTINE
Mistress, it is: sweet lady, entertain him
To be my fellow-servant to your ladyship.

SILVIA
Too low a mistress for so high a servant.

PROTEUS
Not so, sweet lady: but too mean a servant
To have a look of such a worthy mistress.

VALENTINE
Leave off discourse of disability:
Sweet lady, entertain him for your servant.

PROTEUS
My duty will I boast of; nothing else.

SILVIA
And duty never yet did want his meed:
Servant, you are welcome to a worthless mistress.

PROTEUS
I'll die on him that says so but yourself.

SILVIA
That you are welcome?

PROTEUS
That you are worthless.

Re-enter THURIO

THURIO
Madam, my lord your father would speak with you.

SILVIA
I wait upon his pleasure. Come, Sir Thurio,
Go with me. Once more, new servant, welcome:
I'll leave you to confer of home affairs;
When you have done, we look to hear from you.

PROTEUS
We'll both attend upon your ladyship.

Exeunt SILVIA and THURIO

VALENTINE
Now, tell me, how do all from whence you came?

PROTEUS
Your friends are well and have them much
commended.

VALENTINE
And how do yours?

PROTEUS
I left them all in health.

VALENTINE
How does your lady? and how thrives your love?

PROTEUS
My tales of love were wont to weary you;
I know you joy not in a love discourse.

VALENTINE
Ay, Proteus, but that life is alter'd now:
I have done penance for contemning Love,
Whose high imperious thoughts have punish'd me
With bitter fasts, with penitential groans,
With nightly tears and daily heart-sore sighs;
For in revenge of my contempt of love,
Love hath chased sleep from my enthralled eyes
And made them watchers of mine own heart's sorrow.
O gentle Proteus, Love's a mighty lord,
And hath so humbled me, as, I confess,
There is no woe to his correction,
Nor to his service no such joy on earth.
Now no discourse, except it be of love;
Now can I break my fast, dine, sup and sleep,
Upon the very naked name of love.

PROTEUS
Enough; I read your fortune in your eye.
Was this the idol that you worship so?

VALENTINE
Even she; and is she not a heavenly saint?

PROTEUS
No; but she is an earthly paragon.

VALENTINE
Call her divine.

PROTEUS
I will not flatter her.

VALENTINE
O, flatter me; for love delights in praises.

PROTEUS
When I was sick, you gave me bitter pills,
And I must minister the like to you.

VALENTINE
Then speak the truth by her; if not divine,
Yet let her be a principality,
Sovereign to all the creatures on the earth.

PROTEUS
Except my mistress.

VALENTINE
Sweet, except not any;
Except thou wilt except against my love.

PROTEUS
Have I not reason to prefer mine own?

VALENTINE
And I will help thee to prefer her too:
She shall be dignified with this high honour--
To bear my lady's train, lest the base earth
Should from her vesture chance to steal a kiss
And, of so great a favour growing proud,
Disdain to root the summer-swelling flower
And make rough winter everlastingly.

PROTEUS
Why, Valentine, what braggardism is this?

VALENTINE
Pardon me, Proteus: all I can is nothing
To her whose worth makes other worthies nothing;
She is alone.

PROTEUS
Then let her alone.

VALENTINE
Not for the world: why, man, she is mine own,
And I as rich in having such a jewel
As twenty seas, if all their sand were pearl,
The water nectar and the rocks pure gold.
Forgive me that I do not dream on thee,
Because thou see'st me dote upon my love.
My foolish rival, that her father likes
Only for his possessions are so huge,
Is gone with her along, and I must after,
For love, thou know'st, is full of jealousy.

PROTEUS
But she loves you?

VALENTINE
Ay, and we are betroth'd: nay, more, our,
marriage-hour,
With all the cunning manner of our flight,

Determined of; how I must climb her window,
The ladder made of cords, and all the means
Plotted and 'greed on for my happiness.
Good Proteus, go with me to my chamber,
In these affairs to aid me with thy counsel.

PROTEUS
Go on before; I shall inquire you forth:
I must unto the road, to disembark
Some necessaries that I needs must use,
And then I'll presently attend you.

VALENTINE
Will you make haste?

PROTEUS
I will.

Exit VALENTINE

Even as one heat another heat expels,
Or as one nail by strength drives out another,
So the remembrance of my former love
Is by a newer object quite forgotten.
Is it mine, or Valentine's praise,
Her true perfection, or my false transgression,
That makes me reasonless to reason thus?
She is fair; and so is Julia that I love--
That I did love, for now my love is thaw'd;
Which, like a waxen image, 'gainst a fire,
Bears no impression of the thing it was.
Methinks my zeal to Valentine is cold,
And that I love him not as I was wont.
O, but I love his lady too too much,
And that's the reason I love him so little.
How shall I dote on her with more advice,
That thus without advice begin to love her!
'Tis but her picture I have yet beheld,
And that hath dazzled my reason's light;

But when I look on her perfections,
There is no reason but I shall be blind.
If I can cheque my erring love, I will;
If not, to compass her I'll use my skill.

Exit

SCENE V. The same. A street.

Enter SPEED and LAUNCE severally

SPEED
Launce! by mine honesty, welcome to Milan!

LAUNCE
Forswear not thyself, sweet youth, for I am not welcome. I reckon this always, that a man is never undone till he be hanged, nor never welcome to a place till some certain shot be paid and the hostess say 'Welcome!'

SPEED
Come on, you madcap, I'll to the alehouse with you presently; where, for one shot of five pence, thou shalt have five thousand welcomes. But, sirrah, how did thy master part with Madam Julia?

LAUNCE
Marry, after they closed in earnest, they parted very fairly in jest.

SPEED
But shall she marry him?

LAUNCE
No.

SPEED
How then? shall he marry her?

LAUNCE
No, neither.

SPEED
What, are they broken?

LAUNCE
No, they are both as whole as a fish.

SPEED
Why, then, how stands the matter with them?

LAUNCE
Marry, thus: when it stands well with him, it
stands well with her.

SPEED
What an ass art thou! I understand thee not.

LAUNCE
What a block art thou, that thou canst not! My
staff understands me.

SPEED
What thou sayest?

LAUNCE
Ay, and what I do too: look thee, I'll but lean,
and my staff understands me.

SPEED
It stands under thee, indeed.

LAUNCE
Why, stand-under and under-stand is all one.

SPEED
But tell me true, will't be a match?

LAUNCE
Ask my dog: if he say ay, it will! if he say no,
it will; if he shake his tail and say nothing, it will.

SPEED
The conclusion is then that it will.

LAUNCE
Thou shalt never get such a secret from me but by a
parable.

SPEED
'Tis well that I get it so. But, Launce, how sayest
thou, that my master is become a notable lover?

LAUNCE
I never knew him otherwise.

SPEED
Than how?

LAUNCE
A notable lubber, as thou reportest him to be.

SPEED
Why, thou whoreson ass, thou mistakest me.

LAUNCE
Why, fool, I meant not thee; I meant thy master.

SPEED
I tell thee, my master is become a hot lover.

LAUNCE
Why, I tell thee, I care not though he burn himself
in love. If thou wilt, go with me to the alehouse;
if not, thou art an Hebrew, a Jew, and not worth the
name of a Christian.

SPEED
Why?

LAUNCE
Because thou hast not so much charity in thee as to
go to the ale with a Christian. Wilt thou go?

SPEED
At thy service.

Exeunt

SCENE VI. The same. The DUKE'S palace.

Enter PROTEUS

PROTEUS
To leave my Julia, shall I be forsworn;
To love fair Silvia, shall I be forsworn;
To wrong my friend, I shall be much forsworn;
And even that power which gave me first my oath
Provokes me to this threefold perjury;
Love bade me swear and Love bids me forswear.
O sweet-suggesting Love, if thou hast sinned,
Teach me, thy tempted subject, to excuse it!
At first I did adore a twinkling star,
But now I worship a celestial sun.
Unheedful vows may heedfully be broken,
And he wants wit that wants resolved will
To learn his wit to exchange the bad for better.
Fie, fie, unreverend tongue! to call her bad,
Whose sovereignty so oft thou hast preferr'd
With twenty thousand soul-confirming oaths.
I cannot leave to love, and yet I do;
But there I leave to love where I should love.
Julia I lose and Valentine I lose:
If I keep them, I needs must lose myself;
If I lose them, thus find I by their loss
For Valentine myself, for Julia Silvia.
I to myself am dearer than a friend,
For love is still most precious in itself;
And Silvia--witness Heaven, that made her fair!--
Shows Julia but a swarthy Ethiope.
I will forget that Julia is alive,
Remembering that my love to her is dead;
And Valentine I'll hold an enemy,
Aiming at Silvia as a sweeter friend.
I cannot now prove constant to myself,
Without some treachery used to Valentine.
This night he meaneth with a corded ladder

To climb celestial Silvia's chamber-window,
Myself in counsel, his competitor.
Now presently I'll give her father notice
Of their disguising and pretended flight;
Who, all enraged, will banish Valentine;
For Thurio, he intends, shall wed his daughter;
But, Valentine being gone, I'll quickly cross
By some sly trick blunt Thurio's dull proceeding.
Love, lend me wings to make my purpose swift,
As thou hast lent me wit to plot this drift!

Exit

SCENE VII. Verona. JULIA'S house.

Enter JULIA and LUCETTA

JULIA
Counsel, Lucetta; gentle girl, assist me;
And even in kind love I do conjure thee,
Who art the table wherein all my thoughts
Are visibly character'd and engraved,
To lesson me and tell me some good mean
How, with my honour, I may undertake
A journey to my loving Proteus.

LUCETTA
Alas, the way is wearisome and long!

JULIA
A true-devoted pilgrim is not weary
To measure kingdoms with his feeble steps;
Much less shall she that hath Love's wings to fly,
And when the flight is made to one so dear,
Of such divine perfection, as Sir Proteus.

LUCETTA
Better forbear till Proteus make return.

JULIA
O, know'st thou not his looks are my soul's food?
Pity the dearth that I have pined in,
By longing for that food so long a time.
Didst thou but know the inly touch of love,
Thou wouldst as soon go kindle fire with snow
As seek to quench the fire of love with words.

LUCETTA
I do not seek to quench your love's hot fire,
But qualify the fire's extreme rage,
Lest it should burn above the bounds of reason.

JULIA
The more thou damm'st it up, the more it burns.
The current that with gentle murmur glides,
Thou know'st, being stopp'd, impatiently doth rage;
But when his fair course is not hindered,
He makes sweet music with the enamell'd stones,
Giving a gentle kiss to every sedge
He overtaketh in his pilgrimage,
And so by many winding nooks he strays
With willing sport to the wild ocean.
Then let me go and hinder not my course
I'll be as patient as a gentle stream
And make a pastime of each weary step,
Till the last step have brought me to my love;
And there I'll rest, as after much turmoil
A blessed soul doth in Elysium.

LUCETTA
But in what habit will you go along?

JULIA
Not like a woman; for I would prevent
The loose encounters of lascivious men:
Gentle Lucetta, fit me with such weeds
As may beseem some well-reputed page.

LUCETTA
Why, then, your ladyship must cut your hair.

JULIA
No, girl, I'll knit it up in silken strings
With twenty odd-conceited true-love knots.
To be fantastic may become a youth
Of greater time than I shall show to be.

LUCETTA
What fashion, madam shall I make your breeches?

JULIA
That fits as well as 'Tell me, good my lord,
What compass will you wear your farthingale?'
Why even what fashion thou best likest, Lucetta.

LUCETTA
You must needs have them with a codpiece, madam.

JULIA
Out, out, Lucetta! that would be ill-favour'd.

LUCETTA
A round hose, madam, now's not worth a pin,
Unless you have a codpiece to stick pins on.

JULIA
Lucetta, as thou lovest me, let me have
What thou thinkest meet and is most mannerly.
But tell me, wench, how will the world repute me
For undertaking so unstaid a journey?
I fear me, it will make me scandalized.

LUCETTA
If you think so, then stay at home and go not.

JULIA
Nay, that I will not.

LUCETTA
Then never dream on infamy, but go.
If Proteus like your journey when you come,
No matter who's displeased when you are gone:
I fear me, he will scarce be pleased withal.

JULIA
That is the least, Lucetta, of my fear:
A thousand oaths, an ocean of his tears
And instances of infinite of love
Warrant me welcome to my Proteus.

LUCETTA
All these are servants to deceitful men.

JULIA
Base men, that use them to so base effect!
But truer stars did govern Proteus' birth
His words are bonds, his oaths are oracles,
His love sincere, his thoughts immaculate,
His tears pure messengers sent from his heart,
His heart as far from fraud as heaven from earth.

LUCETTA
Pray heaven he prove so, when you come to him!

JULIA
Now, as thou lovest me, do him not that wrong
To bear a hard opinion of his truth:
Only deserve my love by loving him;
And presently go with me to my chamber,
To take a note of what I stand in need of,
To furnish me upon my longing journey.
All that is mine I leave at thy dispose,
My goods, my lands, my reputation;
Only, in lieu thereof, dispatch me hence.
Come, answer not, but to it presently!
I am impatient of my tarriance.

Exeunt

ACT III

SCENE I. Milan. The DUKE's palace.

Enter DUKE, THURIO, and PROTEUS

DUKE
Sir Thurio, give us leave, I pray, awhile;
We have some secrets to confer about.

Exit THURIO

Now, tell me, Proteus, what's your will with me?

PROTEUS
My gracious lord, that which I would discover
The law of friendship bids me to conceal;
But when I call to mind your gracious favours
Done to me, undeserving as I am,
My duty pricks me on to utter that
Which else no worldly good should draw from me.
Know, worthy prince, Sir Valentine, my friend,
This night intends to steal away your daughter:
Myself am one made privy to the plot.
I know you have determined to bestow her
On Thurio, whom your gentle daughter hates;
And should she thus be stol'n away from you,
It would be much vexation to your age.
Thus, for my duty's sake, I rather chose
To cross my friend in his intended drift
Than, by concealing it, heap on your head
A pack of sorrows which would press you down,
Being unprevented, to your timeless grave.

DUKE
Proteus, I thank thee for thine honest care;
Which to requite, command me while I live.

This love of theirs myself have often seen,
Haply when they have judged me fast asleep,
And oftentimes have purposed to forbid
Sir Valentine her company and my court:
But fearing lest my jealous aim might err
And so unworthily disgrace the man,
A rashness that I ever yet have shunn'd,
I gave him gentle looks, thereby to find
That which thyself hast now disclosed to me.
And, that thou mayst perceive my fear of this,
Knowing that tender youth is soon suggested,
I nightly lodge her in an upper tower,
The key whereof myself have ever kept;
And thence she cannot be convey'd away.

PROTEUS
Know, noble lord, they have devised a mean
How he her chamber-window will ascend
And with a corded ladder fetch her down;
For which the youthful lover now is gone
And this way comes he with it presently;
Where, if it please you, you may intercept him.
But, good my Lord, do it so cunningly
That my discovery be not aimed at;
For love of you, not hate unto my friend,
Hath made me publisher of this pretence.

DUKE
Upon mine honour, he shall never know
That I had any light from thee of this.

PROTEUS
Adieu, my Lord; Sir Valentine is coming.

Exit

Enter VALENTINE

DUKE
Sir Valentine, whither away so fast?

VALENTINE
Please it your grace, there is a messenger
That stays to bear my letters to my friends,
And I am going to deliver them.

DUKE
Be they of much import?

VALENTINE
The tenor of them doth but signify
My health and happy being at your court.

DUKE
Nay then, no matter; stay with me awhile;
I am to break with thee of some affairs
That touch me near, wherein thou must be secret.
'Tis not unknown to thee that I have sought
To match my friend Sir Thurio to my daughter.

VALENTINE
I know it well, my Lord; and, sure, the match
Were rich and honourable; besides, the gentleman
Is full of virtue, bounty, worth and qualities
Beseeming such a wife as your fair daughter:
Cannot your Grace win her to fancy him?

DUKE
No, trust me; she is peevish, sullen, froward,
Proud, disobedient, stubborn, lacking duty,
Neither regarding that she is my child
Nor fearing me as if I were her father;
And, may I say to thee, this pride of hers,
Upon advice, hath drawn my love from her;
And, where I thought the remnant of mine age
Should have been cherish'd by her child-like duty,
I now am full resolved to take a wife

And turn her out to who will take her in:
Then let her beauty be her wedding-dower;
For me and my possessions she esteems not.

VALENTINE
What would your Grace have me to do in this?

DUKE
There is a lady in Verona here
Whom I affect; but she is nice and coy
And nought esteems my aged eloquence:
Now therefore would I have thee to my tutor--
For long agone I have forgot to court;
Besides, the fashion of the time is changed--
How and which way I may bestow myself
To be regarded in her sun-bright eye.

VALENTINE
Win her with gifts, if she respect not words:
Dumb jewels often in their silent kind
More than quick words do move a woman's mind.

DUKE
But she did scorn a present that I sent her.

VALENTINE
A woman sometimes scorns what best contents her.
Send her another; never give her o'er;
For scorn at first makes after-love the more.
If she do frown, 'tis not in hate of you,
But rather to beget more love in you:
If she do chide, 'tis not to have you gone;
For why, the fools are mad, if left alone.
Take no repulse, whatever she doth say;
For 'get you gone,' she doth not mean 'away!'
Flatter and praise, commend, extol their graces;
Though ne'er so black, say they have angels' faces.
That man that hath a tongue, I say, is no man,
If with his tongue he cannot win a woman.

DUKE
But she I mean is promised by her friends
Unto a youthful gentleman of worth,
And kept severely from resort of men,
That no man hath access by day to her.

VALENTINE
Why, then, I would resort to her by night.

DUKE
Ay, but the doors be lock'd and keys kept safe,
That no man hath recourse to her by night.

VALENTINE
What lets but one may enter at her window?

DUKE
Her chamber is aloft, far from the ground,
And built so shelving that one cannot climb it
Without apparent hazard of his life.

VALENTINE
Why then, a ladder quaintly made of cords,
To cast up, with a pair of anchoring hooks,
Would serve to scale another Hero's tower,
So bold Leander would adventure it.

DUKE
Now, as thou art a gentleman of blood,
Advise me where I may have such a ladder.

VALENTINE
When would you use it? pray, sir, tell me that.

DUKE
This very night; for Love is like a child,
That longs for every thing that he can come by.

VALENTINE
By seven o'clock I'll get you such a ladder.

DUKE
But, hark thee; I will go to her alone:
How shall I best convey the ladder thither?

VALENTINE
It will be light, my lord, that you may bear it
Under a cloak that is of any length.

DUKE
A cloak as long as thine will serve the turn?

VALENTINE
Ay, my good lord.

DUKE
Then let me see thy cloak:
I'll get me one of such another length.

VALENTINE
Why, any cloak will serve the turn, my lord.

DUKE
How shall I fashion me to wear a cloak?
I pray thee, let me feel thy cloak upon me.
What letter is this same? What's here? 'To Silvia'!
And here an engine fit for my proceeding.
I'll be so bold to break the seal for once.

Reads

'My thoughts do harbour with my Silvia nightly,
And slaves they are to me that send them flying:
O, could their master come and go as lightly,
Himself would lodge where senseless they are lying!
My herald thoughts in thy pure bosom rest them:
While I, their king, that hither them importune,

Do curse the grace that with such grace hath bless'd
them,
Because myself do want my servants' fortune:
I curse myself, for they are sent by me,
That they should harbour where their lord would be.'
What's here?
'Silvia, this night I will enfranchise thee.'
'Tis so; and here's the ladder for the purpose.
Why, Phaeton,--for thou art Merops' son,--
Wilt thou aspire to guide the heavenly car
And with thy daring folly burn the world?
Wilt thou reach stars, because they shine on thee?
Go, base intruder! overweening slave!
Bestow thy fawning smiles on equal mates,
And think my patience, more than thy desert,
Is privilege for thy departure hence:
Thank me for this more than for all the favours
Which all too much I have bestow'd on thee.
But if thou linger in my territories
Longer than swiftest expedition
Will give thee time to leave our royal court,
By heaven! my wrath shall far exceed the love
I ever bore my daughter or thyself.
Be gone! I will not hear thy vain excuse;
But, as thou lovest thy life, make speed from hence.

Exit

VALENTINE
And why not death rather than living torment?
To die is to be banish'd from myself;
And Silvia is myself: banish'd from her
Is self from self: a deadly banishment!
What light is light, if Silvia be not seen?
What joy is joy, if Silvia be not by?
Unless it be to think that she is by
And feed upon the shadow of perfection
Except I be by Silvia in the night,
There is no music in the nightingale;

Unless I look on Silvia in the day,
There is no day for me to look upon;
She is my essence, and I leave to be,
If I be not by her fair influence
Foster'd, illumined, cherish'd, kept alive.
I fly not death, to fly his deadly doom:
Tarry I here, I but attend on death:
But, fly I hence, I fly away from life.

Enter PROTEUS and LAUNCE

PROTEUS
Run, boy, run, run, and seek him out.

LAUNCE
Soho, soho!

PROTEUS
What seest thou?

LAUNCE
Him we go to find: there's not a hair on's head
but 'tis a Valentine.

PROTEUS
Valentine?

VALENTINE
No.

PROTEUS
Who then? his spirit?

VALENTINE
Neither.

PROTEUS
What then?

VALENTINE
Nothing.

LAUNCE
Can nothing speak? Master, shall I strike?

PROTEUS
Who wouldst thou strike?

LAUNCE
Nothing.

PROTEUS
Villain, forbear.

LAUNCE
Why, sir, I'll strike nothing: I pray you,--

PROTEUS
Sirrah, I say, forbear. Friend Valentine, a word.

VALENTINE
My ears are stopt and cannot hear good news,
So much of bad already hath possess'd them.

PROTEUS
Then in dumb silence will I bury mine,
For they are harsh, untuneable and bad.

VALENTINE
Is Silvia dead?

PROTEUS
No, Valentine.

VALENTINE
No Valentine, indeed, for sacred Silvia.
Hath she forsworn me?

PROTEUS
No, Valentine.

VALENTINE
No Valentine, if Silvia have forsworn me.
What is your news?

LAUNCE
Sir, there is a proclamation that you are vanished.

PROTEUS
That thou art banished--O, that's the news!--
From hence, from Silvia and from me thy friend.

VALENTINE
O, I have fed upon this woe already,
And now excess of it will make me surfeit.
Doth Silvia know that I am banished?

PROTEUS
Ay, ay; and she hath offer'd to the doom--
Which, unreversed, stands in effectual force--
A sea of melting pearl, which some call tears:
Those at her father's churlish feet she tender'd;
With them, upon her knees, her humble self;
Wringing her hands, whose whiteness so became them
As if but now they waxed pale for woe:
But neither bended knees, pure hands held up,
Sad sighs, deep groans, nor silver-shedding tears,
Could penetrate her uncompassionate sire;
But Valentine, if he be ta'en, must die.
Besides, her intercession chafed him so,
When she for thy repeal was suppliant,
That to close prison he commanded her,
With many bitter threats of biding there.

VALENTINE
No more; unless the next word that thou speak'st
Have some malignant power upon my life:

If so, I pray thee, breathe it in mine ear,
As ending anthem of my endless dolour.

PROTEUS
Cease to lament for that thou canst not help,
And study help for that which thou lament'st.
Time is the nurse and breeder of all good.
Here if thou stay, thou canst not see thy love;
Besides, thy staying will abridge thy life.
Hope is a lover's staff; walk hence with that
And manage it against despairing thoughts.
Thy letters may be here, though thou art hence;
Which, being writ to me, shall be deliver'd
Even in the milk-white bosom of thy love.
The time now serves not to expostulate:
Come, I'll convey thee through the city-gate;
And, ere I part with thee, confer at large
Of all that may concern thy love-affairs.
As thou lovest Silvia, though not for thyself,
Regard thy danger, and along with me!

VALENTINE
I pray thee, Launce, an if thou seest my boy,
Bid him make haste and meet me at the North-gate.

PROTEUS
Go, sirrah, find him out. Come, Valentine.

VALENTINE
O my dear Silvia! Hapless Valentine!

Exeunt VALENTINE and PROTEUS

LAUNCE
I am but a fool, look you; and yet I have the wit to
think my master is a kind of a knave: but that's
all one, if he be but one knave. He lives not now
that knows me to be in love; yet I am in love; but a
team of horse shall not pluck that from me; nor who

'tis I love; and yet 'tis a woman; but what woman, I
will not tell myself; and yet 'tis a milkmaid; yet
'tis not a maid, for she hath had gossips; yet 'tis
a maid, for she is her master's maid, and serves for
wages. She hath more qualities than a water-spaniel;
which is much in a bare Christian.

Pulling out a paper

Here is the cate-log of her condition.
'Imprimis: She can fetch and carry.' Why, a horse
can do no more: nay, a horse cannot fetch, but only
carry; therefore is she better than a jade. 'Item:
She can milk;' look you, a sweet virtue in a maid
with clean hands.

Enter SPEED

SPEED
How now, Signior Launce! what news with your
mastership?

LAUNCE
With my master's ship? why, it is at sea.

SPEED
Well, your old vice still; mistake the word. What
news, then, in your paper?

LAUNCE
The blackest news that ever thou heardest.

SPEED
Why, man, how black?

LAUNCE
Why, as black as ink.

SPEED
Let me read them.

LAUNCE
Fie on thee, jolt-head! thou canst not read.

SPEED
Thou liest; I can.

LAUNCE
I will try thee. Tell me this: who begot thee?

SPEED
Marry, the son of my grandfather.

LAUNCE
O illiterate loiterer! it was the son of thy
grandmother: this proves that thou canst not read.

SPEED
Come, fool, come; try me in thy paper.

LAUNCE
There; and St. Nicholas be thy speed!

SPEED
[Reads] 'Imprimis: She can milk.'

LAUNCE
Ay, that she can.

SPEED
'Item: She brews good ale.'

LAUNCE
And thereof comes the proverb: 'Blessing of your
heart, you brew good ale.'

SPEED
'Item: She can sew.'

LAUNCE
That's as much as to say, Can she so?

SPEED
'Item: She can knit.'

LAUNCE
What need a man care for a stock with a wench, when
she can knit him a stock?

SPEED
'Item: She can wash and scour.'

LAUNCE
A special virtue: for then she need not be washed
and scoured.

SPEED
'Item: She can spin.'

LAUNCE
Then may I set the world on wheels, when she can
spin for her living.

SPEED
'Item: She hath many nameless virtues.'

LAUNCE
That's as much as to say, bastard virtues; that,
indeed, know not their fathers and therefore have no
names.

SPEED
'Here follow her vices.'

LAUNCE
Close at the heels of her virtues.

SPEED
'Item: She is not to be kissed fasting in respect
of her breath.'

LAUNCE
Well, that fault may be mended with a breakfast. Read
on.

SPEED
'Item: She hath a sweet mouth.'

LAUNCE
That makes amends for her sour breath.

SPEED
'Item: She doth talk in her sleep.'

LAUNCE
It's no matter for that, so she sleep not in her talk.

SPEED
'Item: She is slow in words.'

LAUNCE
O villain, that set this down among her vices! To
be slow in words is a woman's only virtue: I pray
thee, out with't, and place it for her chief virtue.

SPEED
'Item: She is proud.'

LAUNCE
Out with that too; it was Eve's legacy, and cannot
be ta'en from her.

SPEED
'Item: She hath no teeth.'

LAUNCE
I care not for that neither, because I love crusts.

SPEED
'Item: She is curst.'

LAUNCE
Well, the best is, she hath no teeth to bite.

SPEED
'Item: She will often praise her liquor.'

LAUNCE
If her liquor be good, she shall: if she will not, I
will; for good things should be praised.

SPEED
'Item: She is too liberal.'

LAUNCE
Of her tongue she cannot, for that's writ down she
is slow of; of her purse she shall not, for that
I'll keep shut: now, of another thing she may, and
that cannot I help. Well, proceed.

SPEED
'Item: She hath more hair than wit, and more faults
than hairs, and more wealth than faults.'

LAUNCE
Stop there; I'll have her: she was mine, and not
mine, twice or thrice in that last article.
Rehearse that once more.

SPEED
'Item: She hath more hair than wit,'--

LAUNCE
More hair than wit? It may be; I'll prove it. The
cover of the salt hides the salt, and therefore it
is more than the salt; the hair that covers the wit
is more than the wit, for the greater hides the
less. What's next?

SPEED
'And more faults than hairs,'--

LAUNCE
That's monstrous: O, that that were out!

SPEED
'And more wealth than faults.'

LAUNCE
Why, that word makes the faults gracious. Well,
I'll have her; and if it be a match, as nothing is
impossible,--

SPEED
What then?

LAUNCE
Why, then will I tell thee--that thy master stays
for thee at the North-gate.

SPEED
For me?

LAUNCE
For thee! ay, who art thou? he hath stayed for a
better man than thee.

SPEED
And must I go to him?

LAUNCE
Thou must run to him, for thou hast stayed so long
that going will scarce serve the turn.

SPEED
Why didst not tell me sooner? pox of your love letters!

Exit

LAUNCE
Now will he be swinged for reading my letter; an
unmannerly slave, that will thrust himself into
secrets! I'll after, to rejoice in the boy's correction.

Exit

SCENE II. The same. The DUKE's palace.

Enter DUKE and THURIO

DUKE
Sir Thurio, fear not but that she will love you,
Now Valentine is banish'd from her sight.

THURIO
Since his exile she hath despised me most,
Forsworn my company and rail'd at me,
That I am desperate of obtaining her.

DUKE
This weak impress of love is as a figure
Trenched in ice, which with an hour's heat
Dissolves to water and doth lose his form.
A little time will melt her frozen thoughts
And worthless Valentine shall be forgot.

Enter PROTEUS

How now, Sir Proteus! Is your countryman
According to our proclamation gone?

PROTEUS
Gone, my good lord.

DUKE
My daughter takes his going grievously.

PROTEUS
A little time, my lord, will kill that grief.

DUKE
So I believe; but Thurio thinks not so.
Proteus, the good conceit I hold of thee--
For thou hast shown some sign of good desert--

Makes me the better to confer with thee.

PROTEUS
Longer than I prove loyal to your grace
Let me not live to look upon your grace.

DUKE
Thou know'st how willingly I would effect
The match between Sir Thurio and my daughter.

PROTEUS
I do, my lord.

DUKE
And also, I think, thou art not ignorant
How she opposes her against my will

PROTEUS
She did, my lord, when Valentine was here.

DUKE
Ay, and perversely she persevers so.
What might we do to make the girl forget
The love of Valentine and love Sir Thurio?

PROTEUS
The best way is to slander Valentine
With falsehood, cowardice and poor descent,
Three things that women highly hold in hate.

DUKE
Ay, but she'll think that it is spoke in hate.

PROTEUS
Ay, if his enemy deliver it:
Therefore it must with circumstance be spoken
By one whom she esteemeth as his friend.

DUKE
Then you must undertake to slander him.

PROTEUS
And that, my lord, I shall be loath to do:
'Tis an ill office for a gentleman,
Especially against his very friend.

DUKE
Where your good word cannot advantage him,
Your slander never can endamage him;
Therefore the office is indifferent,
Being entreated to it by your friend.

PROTEUS
You have prevail'd, my lord; if I can do it
By ought that I can speak in his dispraise,
She shall not long continue love to him.
But say this weed her love from Valentine,
It follows not that she will love Sir Thurio.

THURIO
Therefore, as you unwind her love from him,
Lest it should ravel and be good to none,
You must provide to bottom it on me;
Which must be done by praising me as much
As you in worth dispraise Sir Valentine.

DUKE
And, Proteus, we dare trust you in this kind,
Because we know, on Valentine's report,
You are already Love's firm votary
And cannot soon revolt and change your mind.
Upon this warrant shall you have access
Where you with Silvia may confer at large;
For she is lumpish, heavy, melancholy,
And, for your friend's sake, will be glad of you;
Where you may temper her by your persuasion
To hate young Valentine and love my friend.

PROTEUS
As much as I can do, I will effect:
But you, Sir Thurio, are not sharp enough;
You must lay lime to tangle her desires
By wailful sonnets, whose composed rhymes
Should be full-fraught with serviceable vows.

DUKE
Ay,
Much is the force of heaven-bred poesy.

PROTEUS
Say that upon the altar of her beauty
You sacrifice your tears, your sighs, your heart:
Write till your ink be dry, and with your tears
Moist it again, and frame some feeling line
That may discover such integrity:
For Orpheus' lute was strung with poets' sinews,
Whose golden touch could soften steel and stones,
Make tigers tame and huge leviathans
Forsake unsounded deeps to dance on sands.
After your dire-lamenting elegies,
Visit by night your lady's chamber-window
With some sweet concert; to their instruments
Tune a deploring dump: the night's dead silence
Will well become such sweet-complaining grievance.
This, or else nothing, will inherit her.

DUKE
This discipline shows thou hast been in love.

THURIO
And thy advice this night I'll put in practise.
Therefore, sweet Proteus, my direction-giver,
Let us into the city presently
To sort some gentlemen well skill'd in music.
I have a sonnet that will serve the turn
To give the onset to thy good advice.

DUKE
About it, gentlemen!

PROTEUS
We'll wait upon your grace till after supper,
And afterward determine our proceedings.

DUKE
Even now about it! I will pardon you.

Exeunt

ACT IV

SCENE I. The frontiers of Mantua. A forest.

Enter certain Outlaws

First Outlaw
Fellows, stand fast; I see a passenger.

Second Outlaw
If there be ten, shrink not, but down with 'em.

Enter VALENTINE and SPEED

Third Outlaw
Stand, sir, and throw us that you have about ye:
If not: we'll make you sit and rifle you.

SPEED
Sir, we are undone; these are the villains
That all the travellers do fear so much.

VALENTINE
My friends,--

First Outlaw
That's not so, sir: we are your enemies.

Second Outlaw
Peace! we'll hear him.

Third Outlaw
Ay, by my beard, will we, for he's a proper man.

VALENTINE
Then know that I have little wealth to lose:
A man I am cross'd with adversity;

My riches are these poor habiliments,
Of which if you should here disfurnish me,
You take the sum and substance that I have.

Second Outlaw
Whither travel you?

VALENTINE
To Verona.

First Outlaw
Whence came you?

VALENTINE
From Milan.

Third Outlaw
Have you long sojourned there?

VALENTINE
Some sixteen months, and longer might have stay'd,
If crooked fortune had not thwarted me.

First Outlaw
What, were you banish'd thence?

VALENTINE
I was.

Second Outlaw
For what offence?

VALENTINE
For that which now torments me to rehearse:
I kill'd a man, whose death I much repent;
Bu t yet I slew him manfully in fight,
Without false vantage or base treachery.

First Outlaw
Why, ne'er repent it, if it were done so.
But were you banish'd for so small a fault?

VALENTINE
I was, and held me glad of such a doom.

Second Outlaw
Have you the tongues?

VALENTINE
My youthful travel therein made me happy,
Or else I often had been miserable.

Third Outlaw
By the bare scalp of Robin Hood's fat friar,
This fellow were a king for our wild faction!

First Outlaw
We'll have him. Sirs, a word.

SPEED
Master, be one of them; it's an honourable kind of
thievery.

VALENTINE
Peace, villain!

Second Outlaw
Tell us this: have you any thing to take to?

VALENTINE
Nothing but my fortune.

Third Outlaw
Know, then, that some of us are gentlemen,
Such as the fury of ungovern'd youth
Thrust from the company of awful men:
Myself was from Verona banished

For practising to steal away a lady,
An heir, and near allied unto the duke.

Second Outlaw
And I from Mantua, for a gentleman,
Who, in my mood, I stabb'd unto the heart.

First Outlaw
And I for such like petty crimes as these,
But to the purpose--for we cite our faults,
That they may hold excus'd our lawless lives;
And partly, seeing you are beautified
With goodly shape and by your own report
A linguist and a man of such perfection
As we do in our quality much want--

Second Outlaw
Indeed, because you are a banish'd man,
Therefore, above the rest, we parley to you:
Are you content to be our general?
To make a virtue of necessity
And live, as we do, in this wilderness?

Third Outlaw
What say'st thou? wilt thou be of our consort?
Say ay, and be the captain of us all:
We'll do thee homage and be ruled by thee,
Love thee as our commander and our king.

First Outlaw
But if thou scorn our courtesy, thou diest.

Second Outlaw
Thou shalt not live to brag what we have offer'd.

VALENTINE
I take your offer and will live with you,
Provided that you do no outrages
On silly women or poor passengers.

Third Outlaw
No, we detest such vile base practises.
Come, go with us, we'll bring thee to our crews,
And show thee all the treasure we have got,
Which, with ourselves, all rest at thy dispose.

Exeunt

SCENE II. Milan. Outside the DUKE's palace, under SILVIA's chamber.

Enter PROTEUS

PROTEUS
Already have I been false to Valentine
And now I must be as unjust to Thurio.
Under the colour of commending him,
I have access my own love to prefer:
But Silvia is too fair, too true, too holy,
To be corrupted with my worthless gifts.
When I protest true loyalty to her,
She twits me with my falsehood to my friend;
When to her beauty I commend my vows,
She bids me think how I have been forsworn
In breaking faith with Julia whom I loved:
And notwithstanding all her sudden quips,
The least whereof would quell a lover's hope,
Yet, spaniel-like, the more she spurns my love,
The more it grows and fawneth on her still.
But here comes Thurio: now must we to her window,
And give some evening music to her ear.

Enter THURIO and Musicians

THURIO
How now, Sir Proteus, are you crept before us?

PROTEUS
Ay, gentle Thurio: for you know that love
Will creep in service where it cannot go.

THURIO
Ay, but I hope, sir, that you love not here.

PROTEUS
Sir, but I do; or else I would be hence.

THURIO
Who? Silvia?

PROTEUS
Ay, Silvia; for your sake.

THURIO
I thank you for your own. Now, gentlemen,
Let's tune, and to it lustily awhile.

Enter, at a distance, Host, and JULIA in boy's clothes

Host
Now, my young guest, methinks you're allycholly: I
pray you, why is it?

JULIA
Marry, mine host, because I cannot be merry.

Host
Come, we'll have you merry: I'll bring you where
you shall hear music and see the gentleman that you
asked for.

JULIA
But shall I hear him speak?

Host
Ay, that you shall.

JULIA
That will be music.

Music plays

Host
Hark, hark!

JULIA
Is he among these?

Host
Ay: but, peace! let's hear 'em.
SONG.
Who is Silvia? what is she,
That all our swains commend her?
Holy, fair and wise is she;
The heaven such grace did lend her,
That she might admired be.
Is she kind as she is fair?
For beauty lives with kindness.
Love doth to her eyes repair,
To help him of his blindness,
And, being help'd, inhabits there.
Then to Silvia let us sing,
That Silvia is excelling;
She excels each mortal thing
Upon the dull earth dwelling:
To her let us garlands bring.

Host
How now! are you sadder than you were before? How
do you, man? the music likes you not.

JULIA
You mistake; the musician likes me not.

Host
Why, my pretty youth?

JULIA
He plays false, father.

Host
How? out of tune on the strings?

JULIA
Not so; but yet so false that he grieves my very
heart-strings.

Host
You have a quick ear.

JULIA
Ay, I would I were deaf; it makes me have a slow
heart.

Host
I perceive you delight not in music.

JULIA
Not a whit, when it jars so.

Host
Hark, what fine change is in the music!

JULIA
Ay, that change is the spite.

Host
You would have them always play but one thing?

JULIA
I would always have one play but one thing.
But, host, doth this Sir Proteus that we talk on
Often resort unto this gentlewoman?

Host
I tell you what Launce, his man, told me: he loved
her out of all nick.

JULIA
Where is Launce?

Host
Gone to seek his dog; which tomorrow, by his
master's command, he must carry for a present to his
lady.

JULIA
Peace! stand aside: the company parts.

PROTEUS
Sir Thurio, fear not you: I will so plead
That you shall say my cunning drift excels.

THURIO
Where meet we?

PROTEUS
At Saint Gregory's well.

THURIO
Farewell.

Exeunt THURIO and Musicians

Enter SILVIA above

PROTEUS
Madam, good even to your ladyship.

SILVIA
I thank you for your music, gentlemen.
Who is that that spake?

PROTEUS
One, lady, if you knew his pure heart's truth,
You would quickly learn to know him by his voice.

SILVIA
Sir Proteus, as I take it.

PROTEUS
Sir Proteus, gentle lady, and your servant.

SILVIA
What's your will?

PROTEUS
That I may compass yours.

SILVIA
You have your wish; my will is even this:
That presently you hie you home to bed.
Thou subtle, perjured, false, disloyal man!
Think'st thou I am so shallow, so conceitless,
To be seduced by thy flattery,
That hast deceived so many with thy vows?
Return, return, and make thy love amends.
For me, by this pale queen of night I swear,
I am so far from granting thy request
That I despise thee for thy wrongful suit,
And by and by intend to chide myself
Even for this time I spend in talking to thee.

PROTEUS
I grant, sweet love, that I did love a lady;
But she is dead.

JULIA
[Aside] 'Twere false, if I should speak it;
For I am sure she is not buried.

SILVIA
Say that she be; yet Valentine thy friend
Survives; to whom, thyself art witness,
I am betroth'd: and art thou not ashamed
To wrong him with thy importunacy?

PROTEUS
I likewise hear that Valentine is dead.

SILVIA
And so suppose am I; for in his grave
Assure thyself my love is buried.

PROTEUS
Sweet lady, let me rake it from the earth.

SILVIA
Go to thy lady's grave and call hers thence,
Or, at the least, in hers sepulchre thine.

JULIA
[Aside] He heard not that.

PROTEUS
Madam, if your heart be so obdurate,
Vouchsafe me yet your picture for my love,
The picture that is hanging in your chamber;
To that I'll speak, to that I'll sigh and weep:
For since the substance of your perfect self
Is else devoted, I am but a shadow;
And to your shadow will I make true love.

JULIA
[Aside] If 'twere a substance, you would, sure, deceive it,
And make it but a shadow, as I am.

SILVIA
I am very loath to be your idol, sir;
But since your falsehood shall become you well
To worship shadows and adore false shapes,
Send to me in the morning and I'll send it:
And so, good rest.

PROTEUS
As wretches have o'ernight
That wait for execution in the morn.

Exeunt PROTEUS and SILVIA severally

JULIA
Host, will you go?

Host
By my halidom, I was fast asleep.

JULIA
Pray you, where lies Sir Proteus?

Host
Marry, at my house. Trust me, I think 'tis almost
day.

JULIA
Not so; but it hath been the longest night
That e'er I watch'd and the most heaviest.

Exeunt

SCENE III. The same.

Enter EGLAMOUR

EGLAMOUR
This is the hour that Madam Silvia
Entreated me to call and know her mind:
There's some great matter she'ld employ me in.
Madam, madam!

Enter SILVIA above

SILVIA
Who calls?

EGLAMOUR
Your servant and your friend;
One that attends your ladyship's command.

SILVIA
Sir Eglamour, a thousand times good morrow.

EGLAMOUR
As many, worthy lady, to yourself:
According to your ladyship's impose,
I am thus early come to know what service
It is your pleasure to command me in.

SILVIA
O Eglamour, thou art a gentleman--
Think not I flatter, for I swear I do not--
Valiant, wise, remorseful, well accomplish'd:
Thou art not ignorant what dear good will
I bear unto the banish'd Valentine,
Nor how my father would enforce me marry
Vain Thurio, whom my very soul abhors.
Thyself hast loved; and I have heard thee say
No grief did ever come so near thy heart

As when thy lady and thy true love died,
Upon whose grave thou vow'dst pure chastity.
Sir Eglamour, I would to Valentine,
To Mantua, where I hear he makes abode;
And, for the ways are dangerous to pass,
I do desire thy worthy company,
Upon whose faith and honour I repose.
Urge not my father's anger, Eglamour,
But think upon my grief, a lady's grief,
And on the justice of my flying hence,
To keep me from a most unholy match,
Which heaven and fortune still rewards with plagues.
I do desire thee, even from a heart
As full of sorrows as the sea of sands,
To bear me company and go with me:
If not, to hide what I have said to thee,
That I may venture to depart alone.

EGLAMOUR
Madam, I pity much your grievances;
Which since I know they virtuously are placed,
I give consent to go along with you,
Recking as little what betideth me
As much I wish all good befortune you.
When will you go?

SILVIA
This evening coming.

EGLAMOUR
Where shall I meet you?

SILVIA
At Friar Patrick's cell,
Where I intend holy confession.

EGLAMOUR
I will not fail your ladyship. Good morrow, gentle lady.

SILVIA
Good morrow, kind Sir Eglamour.

Exeunt severally

SCENE IV. The same.

Enter LAUNCE, with his his Dog

LAUNCE
When a man's servant shall play the cur with him,
look you, it goes hard: one that I brought up of a
puppy; one that I saved from drowning, when three or
four of his blind brothers and sisters went to it.
I have taught him, even as one would say precisely,
'thus I would teach a dog.' I was sent to deliver
him as a present to Mistress Silvia from my master;
and I came no sooner into the dining-chamber but he
steps me to her trencher and steals her capon's leg:
O, 'tis a foul thing when a cur cannot keep himself
in all companies! I would have, as one should say,
one that takes upon him to be a dog indeed, to be,
as it were, a dog at all things. If I had not had
more wit than he, to take a fault upon me that he did,
I think verily he had been hanged for't; sure as I
live, he had suffered for't; you shall judge. He
thrusts me himself into the company of three or four
gentlemanlike dogs under the duke's table: he had
not been there--bless the mark!--a pissing while, but
all the chamber smelt him. 'Out with the dog!' says
one: 'What cur is that?' says another: 'Whip him
out' says the third: 'Hang him up' says the duke.
I, having been acquainted with the smell before,
knew it was Crab, and goes me to the fellow that
whips the dogs: 'Friend,' quoth I, 'you mean to whip
the dog?' 'Ay, marry, do I,' quoth he. 'You do him
the more wrong,' quoth I; ''twas I did the thing you
wot of.' He makes me no more ado, but whips me out
of the chamber. How many masters would do this for
his servant? Nay, I'll be sworn, I have sat in the
stocks for puddings he hath stolen, otherwise he had
been executed; I have stood on the pillory for geese
he hath killed, otherwise he had suffered for't.

Thou thinkest not of this now. Nay, I remember the trick you served me when I took my leave of Madam Silvia: did not I bid thee still mark me and do as I do? when didst thou see me heave up my leg and make
water against a gentlewoman's farthingale? didst thou ever see me do such a trick?

Enter PROTEUS and JULIA

PROTEUS
Sebastian is thy name? I like thee well
And will employ thee in some service presently.

JULIA
In what you please: I'll do what I can.

PROTEUS
I hope thou wilt.

To LAUNCE

How now, you whoreson peasant!
Where have you been these two days loitering?

LAUNCE
Marry, sir, I carried Mistress Silvia the dog you bade me.

PROTEUS
And what says she to my little jewel?

LAUNCE
Marry, she says your dog was a cur, and tells you currish thanks is good enough for such a present.

PROTEUS
But she received my dog?

LAUNCE
No, indeed, did she not: here have I brought him
back again.

PROTEUS
What, didst thou offer her this from me?

LAUNCE
Ay, sir: the other squirrel was stolen from me by
the hangman boys in the market-place: and then I
offered her mine own, who is a dog as big as ten of
yours, and therefore the gift the greater.

PROTEUS
Go get thee hence, and find my dog again,
Or ne'er return again into my sight.
Away, I say! stay'st thou to vex me here?

Exit LAUNCE

A slave, that still an end turns me to shame!
Sebastian, I have entertained thee,
Partly that I have need of such a youth
That can with some discretion do my business,
For 'tis no trusting to yond foolish lout,
But chiefly for thy face and thy behavior,
Which, if my augury deceive me not,
Witness good bringing up, fortune and truth:
Therefore know thou, for this I entertain thee.
Go presently and take this ring with thee,
Deliver it to Madam Silvia:
She loved me well deliver'd it to me.

JULIA
It seems you loved not her, to leave her token.
She is dead, belike?

PROTEUS
Not so; I think she lives.

JULIA
Alas!

PROTEUS
Why dost thou cry 'alas'?

JULIA
I cannot choose
But pity her.

PROTEUS
Wherefore shouldst thou pity her?

JULIA
Because methinks that she loved you as well
As you do love your lady Silvia:
She dreams of him that has forgot her love;
You dote on her that cares not for your love.
'Tis pity love should be so contrary;
And thinking of it makes me cry 'alas!'

PROTEUS
Well, give her that ring and therewithal
This letter. That's her chamber. Tell my lady
I claim the promise for her heavenly picture.
Your message done, hie home unto my chamber,
Where thou shalt find me, sad and solitary.

Exit

JULIA
How many women would do such a message?
Alas, poor Proteus! thou hast entertain'd
A fox to be the shepherd of thy lambs.
Alas, poor fool! why do I pity him
That with his very heart despiseth me?
Because he loves her, he despiseth me;
Because I love him I must pity him.

This ring I gave him when he parted from me,
To bind him to remember my good will;
And now am I, unhappy messenger,
To plead for that which I would not obtain,
To carry that which I would have refused,
To praise his faith which I would have dispraised.
I am my master's true-confirmed love;
But cannot be true servant to my master,
Unless I prove false traitor to myself.
Yet will I woo for him, but yet so coldly
As, heaven it knows, I would not have him speed.

Enter SILVIA, attended

Gentlewoman, good day! I pray you, be my mean
To bring me where to speak with Madam Silvia.

SILVIA
What would you with her, if that I be she?

JULIA
If you be she, I do entreat your patience
To hear me speak the message I am sent on.

SILVIA
From whom?

JULIA
From my master, Sir Proteus, madam.

SILVIA
O, he sends you for a picture.

JULIA
Ay, madam.

SILVIA
Ursula, bring my picture here.
Go give your master this: tell him from me,

One Julia, that his changing thoughts forget,
Would better fit his chamber than this shadow.

JULIA
Madam, please you peruse this letter.--
Pardon me, madam; I have unadvised
Deliver'd you a paper that I should not:
This is the letter to your ladyship.

SILVIA
I pray thee, let me look on that again.

JULIA
It may not be; good madam, pardon me.

SILVIA
There, hold!
I will not look upon your master's lines:
I know they are stuff'd with protestations
And full of new-found oaths; which he will break
As easily as I do tear his paper.

JULIA
Madam, he sends your ladyship this ring.

SILVIA
The more shame for him that he sends it me;
For I have heard him say a thousand times
His Julia gave it him at his departure.
Though his false finger have profaned the ring,
Mine shall not do his Julia so much wrong.

JULIA
She thanks you.

SILVIA
What say'st thou?

JULIA
I thank you, madam, that you tender her.
Poor gentlewoman! my master wrongs her much.

SILVIA
Dost thou know her?

JULIA
Almost as well as I do know myself:
To think upon her woes I do protest
That I have wept a hundred several times.

SILVIA
Belike she thinks that Proteus hath forsook her.

JULIA
I think she doth; and that's her cause of sorrow.

SILVIA
Is she not passing fair?

JULIA
She hath been fairer, madam, than she is:
When she did think my master loved her well,
She, in my judgment, was as fair as you:
But since she did neglect her looking-glass
And threw her sun-expelling mask away,
The air hath starved the roses in her cheeks
And pinch'd the lily-tincture of her face,
That now she is become as black as I.

SILVIA
How tall was she?

JULIA
About my stature; for at Pentecost,
When all our pageants of delight were play'd,
Our youth got me to play the woman's part,
And I was trimm'd in Madam Julia's gown,

Which served me as fit, by all men's judgments,
As if the garment had been made for me:
Therefore I know she is about my height.
And at that time I made her weep agood,
For I did play a lamentable part:
Madam, 'twas Ariadne passioning
For Theseus' perjury and unjust flight;
Which I so lively acted with my tears
That my poor mistress, moved therewithal,
Wept bitterly; and would I might be dead
If I in thought felt not her very sorrow!

SILVIA
She is beholding to thee, gentle youth.
Alas, poor lady, desolate and left!
I weep myself to think upon thy words.
Here, youth, there is my purse; I give thee this
For thy sweet mistress' sake, because thou lovest her.
Farewell.

Exit SILVIA, with attendants

JULIA
And she shall thank you for't, if e'er you know her.
A virtuous gentlewoman, mild and beautiful
I hope my master's suit will be but cold,
Since she respects my mistress' love so much.
Alas, how love can trifle with itself!
Here is her picture: let me see; I think,
If I had such a tire, this face of mine
Were full as lovely as is this of hers:
And yet the painter flatter'd her a little,
Unless I flatter with myself too much.
Her hair is auburn, mine is perfect yellow:
If that be all the difference in his love,
I'll get me such a colour'd periwig.
Her eyes are grey as glass, and so are mine:
Ay, but her forehead's low, and mine's as high.
What should it be that he respects in her

But I can make respective in myself,
If this fond Love were not a blinded god?
Come, shadow, come and take this shadow up,
For 'tis thy rival. O thou senseless form,
Thou shalt be worshipp'd, kiss'd, loved and adored!
And, were there sense in his idolatry,
My substance should be statue in thy stead.
I'll use thee kindly for thy mistress' sake,
That used me so; or else, by Jove I vow,
I should have scratch'd out your unseeing eyes
To make my master out of love with thee!

Exit

ACT V

SCENE I. Milan. An abbey.

Enter EGLAMOUR

EGLAMOUR
The sun begins to gild the western sky;
And now it is about the very hour
That Silvia, at Friar Patrick's cell, should meet me.
She will not fail, for lovers break not hours,
Unless it be to come before their time;
So much they spur their expedition.
See where she comes.

Enter SILVIA

Lady, a happy evening!

SILVIA
Amen, amen! Go on, good Eglamour,
Out at the postern by the abbey-wall:
I fear I am attended by some spies.

EGLAMOUR
Fear not: the forest is not three leagues off;
If we recover that, we are sure enough.

Exeunt

SCENE II. The same. The DUKE's palace.

Enter THURIO, PROTEUS, and JULIA

THURIO
Sir Proteus, what says Silvia to my suit?

PROTEUS
O, sir, I find her milder than she was;
And yet she takes exceptions at your person.

THURIO
What, that my leg is too long?

PROTEUS
No; that it is too little.

THURIO
I'll wear a boot, to make it somewhat rounder.

JULIA
[Aside] But love will not be spurr'd to what
it loathes.

THURIO
What says she to my face?

PROTEUS
She says it is a fair one.

THURIO
Nay then, the wanton lies; my face is black.

PROTEUS
But pearls are fair; and the old saying is,
Black men are pearls in beauteous ladies' eyes.

JULIA
[Aside] 'Tis true; such pearls as put out
ladies' eyes;
For I had rather wink than look on them.

THURIO
How likes she my discourse?

PROTEUS
Ill, when you talk of war.

THURIO
But well, when I discourse of love and peace?

JULIA
[Aside] But better, indeed, when you hold your peace.

THURIO
What says she to my valour?

PROTEUS
O, sir, she makes no doubt of that.

JULIA
[Aside] She needs not, when she knows it cowardice.

THURIO
What says she to my birth?

PROTEUS
That you are well derived.

JULIA
[Aside] True; from a gentleman to a fool.

THURIO
Considers she my possessions?

PROTEUS
O, ay; and pities them.

THURIO
Wherefore?

JULIA
[Aside] That such an ass should owe them.

PROTEUS
That they are out by lease.

JULIA
Here comes the duke.

Enter DUKE

DUKE
How now, Sir Proteus! how now, Thurio!
Which of you saw Sir Eglamour of late?

THURIO
Not I.

PROTEUS
Nor I.

DUKE
Saw you my daughter?

PROTEUS
Neither.

DUKE
Why then,
She's fled unto that peasant Valentine;
And Eglamour is in her company.
'Tis true; for Friar Laurence met them both,
As he in penance wander'd through the forest;

Him he knew well, and guess'd that it was she,
But, being mask'd, he was not sure of it;
Besides, she did intend confession
At Patrick's cell this even; and there she was not;
These likelihoods confirm her flight from hence.
Therefore, I pray you, stand not to discourse,
But mount you presently and meet with me
Upon the rising of the mountain-foot
That leads towards Mantua, whither they are fled:
Dispatch, sweet gentlemen, and follow me.

Exit

THURIO
Why, this it is to be a peevish girl,
That flies her fortune when it follows her.
I'll after, more to be revenged on Eglamour
Than for the love of reckless Silvia.

Exit

PROTEUS
And I will follow, more for Silvia's love
Than hate of Eglamour that goes with her.

Exit

JULIA
And I will follow, more to cross that love
Than hate for Silvia that is gone for love.

Exit

SCENE III. The frontiers of Mantua. The forest.

Enter Outlaws with SILVIA

First Outlaw
Come, come,
Be patient; we must bring you to our captain.

SILVIA
A thousand more mischances than this one
Have learn'd me how to brook this patiently.

Second Outlaw
Come, bring her away.

First Outlaw
Where is the gentleman that was with her?

Third Outlaw
Being nimble-footed, he hath outrun us,
But Moyses and Valerius follow him.
Go thou with her to the west end of the wood;
There is our captain: we'll follow him that's fled;
The thicket is beset; he cannot 'scape.

First Outlaw
Come, I must bring you to our captain's cave:
Fear not; he bears an honourable mind,
And will not use a woman lawlessly.

SILVIA
O Valentine, this I endure for thee!

Exeunt

SCENE IV. Another part of the forest.

Enter VALENTINE

VALENTINE
How use doth breed a habit in a man!
This shadowy desert, unfrequented woods,
I better brook than flourishing peopled towns:
Here can I sit alone, unseen of any,
And to the nightingale's complaining notes
Tune my distresses and record my woes.
O thou that dost inhabit in my breast,
Leave not the mansion so long tenantless,
Lest, growing ruinous, the building fall
And leave no memory of what it was!
Repair me with thy presence, Silvia;
Thou gentle nymph, cherish thy forlorn swain!
What halloing and what stir is this to-day?
These are my mates, that make their wills their law,
Have some unhappy passenger in chase.
They love me well; yet I have much to do
To keep them from uncivil outrages.
Withdraw thee, Valentine: who's this comes here?

Enter PROTEUS, SILVIA, and JULIA

PROTEUS
Madam, this service I have done for you,
Though you respect not aught your servant doth,
To hazard life and rescue you from him
That would have forced your honour and your love;
Vouchsafe me, for my meed, but one fair look;
A smaller boon than this I cannot beg
And less than this, I am sure, you cannot give.

VALENTINE
[Aside] How like a dream is this I see and hear!
Love, lend me patience to forbear awhile.

SILVIA
O miserable, unhappy that I am!

PROTEUS
Unhappy were you, madam, ere I came;
But by my coming I have made you happy.

SILVIA
By thy approach thou makest me most unhappy.

JULIA
[Aside] And me, when he approacheth to your
presence.

SILVIA
Had I been seized by a hungry lion,
I would have been a breakfast to the beast,
Rather than have false Proteus rescue me.
O, Heaven be judge how I love Valentine,
Whose life's as tender to me as my soul!
And full as much, for more there cannot be,
I do detest false perjured Proteus.
Therefore be gone; solicit me no more.

PROTEUS
What dangerous action, stood it next to death,
Would I not undergo for one calm look!
O, 'tis the curse in love, and still approved,
When women cannot love where they're beloved!

SILVIA
When Proteus cannot love where he's beloved.
Read over Julia's heart, thy first best love,
For whose dear sake thou didst then rend thy faith
Into a thousand oaths; and all those oaths
Descended into perjury, to love me.
Thou hast no faith left now, unless thou'dst two;
And that's far worse than none; better have none

Than plural faith which is too much by one:
Thou counterfeit to thy true friend!

PROTEUS
In love
Who respects friend?

SILVIA
All men but Proteus.

PROTEUS
Nay, if the gentle spirit of moving words
Can no way change you to a milder form,
I'll woo you like a soldier, at arms' end,
And love you 'gainst the nature of love,--force ye.

SILVIA
O heaven!

PROTEUS
I'll force thee yield to my desire.

VALENTINE
Ruffian, let go that rude uncivil touch,
Thou friend of an ill fashion!

PROTEUS
Valentine!

VALENTINE
Thou common friend, that's without faith or love,
For such is a friend now; treacherous man!
Thou hast beguiled my hopes; nought but mine eye
Could have persuaded me: now I dare not say
I have one friend alive; thou wouldst disprove me.
Who should be trusted, when one's own right hand
Is perjured to the bosom? Proteus,
I am sorry I must never trust thee more,
But count the world a stranger for thy sake.

The private wound is deepest: O time most accurst,
'Mongst all foes that a friend should be the worst!

PROTEUS
My shame and guilt confounds me.
Forgive me, Valentine: if hearty sorrow
Be a sufficient ransom for offence,
I tender 't here; I do as truly suffer
As e'er I did commit.

VALENTINE
Then I am paid;
And once again I do receive thee honest.
Who by repentance is not satisfied
Is nor of heaven nor earth, for these are pleased.
By penitence the Eternal's wrath's appeased:
And, that my love may appear plain and free,
All that was mine in Silvia I give thee.

JULIA
O me unhappy!

Swoons

PROTEUS
Look to the boy.

VALENTINE
Why, boy! why, wag! how now! what's the matter?
Look up; speak.

JULIA
O good sir, my master charged me to deliver a ring
to Madam Silvia, which, out of my neglect, was never
done.

PROTEUS
Where is that ring, boy?

JULIA
Here 'tis; this is it.

PROTEUS
How! let me see:
Why, this is the ring I gave to Julia.

JULIA
O, cry you mercy, sir, I have mistook:
This is the ring you sent to Silvia.

PROTEUS
But how camest thou by this ring? At my depart
I gave this unto Julia.

JULIA
And Julia herself did give it me;
And Julia herself hath brought it hither.

PROTEUS
How! Julia!

JULIA
Behold her that gave aim to all thy oaths,
And entertain'd 'em deeply in her heart.
How oft hast thou with perjury cleft the root!
O Proteus, let this habit make thee blush!
Be thou ashamed that I have took upon me
Such an immodest raiment, if shame live
In a disguise of love:
It is the lesser blot, modesty finds,
Women to change their shapes than men their minds.

PROTEUS
Than men their minds! 'tis true.
O heaven! were man
But constant, he were perfect. That one error
Fills him with faults; makes him run through all the
sins:

Inconstancy falls off ere it begins.
What is in Silvia's face, but I may spy
More fresh in Julia's with a constant eye?

VALENTINE
Come, come, a hand from either:
Let me be blest to make this happy close;
'Twere pity two such friends should be long foes.

PROTEUS
Bear witness, Heaven, I have my wish for ever.

JULIA
And I mine.

Enter Outlaws, with DUKE and THURIO

Outlaws
A prize, a prize, a prize!

VALENTINE
Forbear, forbear, I say! it is my lord the duke.
Your grace is welcome to a man disgraced,
Banished Valentine.

DUKE
Sir Valentine!

THURIO
Yonder is Silvia; and Silvia's mine.

VALENTINE
Thurio, give back, or else embrace thy death;
Come not within the measure of my wrath;
Do not name Silvia thine; if once again,
Verona shall not hold thee. Here she stands;
Take but possession of her with a touch:
I dare thee but to breathe upon my love.

THURIO
Sir Valentine, I care not for her, I;
I hold him but a fool that will endanger
His body for a girl that loves him not:
I claim her not, and therefore she is thine.

DUKE
The more degenerate and base art thou,
To make such means for her as thou hast done
And leave her on such slight conditions.
Now, by the honour of my ancestry,
I do applaud thy spirit, Valentine,
And think thee worthy of an empress' love:
Know then, I here forget all former griefs,
Cancel all grudge, repeal thee home again,
Plead a new state in thy unrivall'd merit,
To which I thus subscribe: Sir Valentine,
Thou art a gentleman and well derived;
Take thou thy Silvia, for thou hast deserved her.

VALENTINE
I thank your grace; the gift hath made me happy.
I now beseech you, for your daughter's sake,
To grant one boom that I shall ask of you.

DUKE
I grant it, for thine own, whate'er it be.

VALENTINE
These banish'd men that I have kept withal
Are men endued with worthy qualities:
Forgive them what they have committed here
And let them be recall'd from their exile:
They are reformed, civil, full of good
And fit for great employment, worthy lord.

DUKE
Thou hast prevail'd; I pardon them and thee:
Dispose of them as thou know'st their deserts.

Come, let us go: we will include all jars
With triumphs, mirth and rare solemnity.

VALENTINE
And, as we walk along, I dare be bold
With our discourse to make your grace to smile.
What think you of this page, my lord?

DUKE
I think the boy hath grace in him; he blushes.

VALENTINE
I warrant you, my lord, more grace than boy.

DUKE
What mean you by that saying?

VALENTINE
Please you, I'll tell you as we pass along,
That you will wonder what hath fortuned.
Come, Proteus; 'tis your penance but to hear
The story of your loves discovered:
That done, our day of marriage shall be yours;
One feast, one house, one mutual happiness.

Exeunt

CPSIA information can be obtained
at www.ICGtesting.com
Printed in the USA
LVOW12s1608220916

505792LV00002B/287/P